The **Jewish** Mama's Kitchen

Special thanks

I would like to dedicate this book to my mum and dad, who
have always been there for me and to whom I owe so much.

Thunder Bay Press
An imprint of the Advantage Publishers Group
5880 Oberlin Drive, San Diego, CA 92121-4794
www.thunderbaybooks.com

Copyright © MQ Publications Limited, 2005
Text copyright © Denise Phillips, 2005

All notations of errors or omissions should be addressed to Thunder Bay Press, Editorial Department,
at the above address. All other correspondence (author inquiries, permissions) concerning the content
of this book should be addressed to MQ Publications Limited, 12 The Ivories, 6–8 Northampton Street,
London N1 2HY, England. E-mail: mail@mqpublications.com.

Library of Congress Cataloging-in-Publication Data
Phillips, Denise.
    The Jewish Mama's kitchen : authentic homestyle recipes / Denise Phillips.
       p. cm.
     ISBN 1-59223-410-0
       1. Cookery, Jewish. I. Title.

TX724.P483 2005
641.5'676--dc22

2005043062

Printed and bound in China.

1 2 3 4 5   09 08 07 06 05

The Jewish Mama's Kitchen

Authentic homestyle recipes

Denise Phillips

Thunder Bay
P·R·E·S·S

San Diego, California

Acknowledgments

Being called a Jewish mama is a privilege that not all Jewish women are entitled to. But my mother more than deserves it. She sparked my initial interest in cooking as a child, and she has continued to be so supportive right up to this day. I speak to her at least once a day, and over the past few months I have spent many hours discussing and revising many of her recipes for this book. It certainly provided my mother a welcome distraction from worrying about my father, who had been ill, but who has now, thankfully, recovered. I would also like to acknowledge the contribution of two other mamas of my mother's generation—Freda Skovron and Yehudhit Solomans—who provided plenty of ideas for recipes based on their own childhood experiences. In addition, Sharon Feldman-Vazan helped to balance the content of this book by inspiring me to add a number of interesting Sephardi recipes.

The creation of this book occurred at a very busy time in my life and was made possible only by the support of some key people. I would like to thank my friend Marsha Schultz for her time and effort in editing my efforts, and Masa Segota, my au pair, for all her help with food preparation and cleaning up that enabled me to get on with the next recipe. My close friend Lynne Misner was there to help me bounce around ideas and to confirm my train of thought.

Finally, I would like to thank my new husband, Jeremy, for his help in reading through the recipes and providing his input as a complete cooking novice.

And of course, thanks to my children, Abbie, Samantha, and Nick, for getting on and dealing with their homework while I was busy chopping onions and frying fish!

Contents

Introduction

As one of four daughters whose mother and grandmother (as well as a large group of aunts) all loved to cook and entertain, perhaps it was inevitable that I would develop a passion for cooking when I was very young. I was hooked by the way the women all worked together in the kitchen—gossiping, singing, laughing, and crying (from the onions!) as they peeled and chopped, sifted and sorted, melted and measured (not very accurately—they worked by instinct), and stuffed and grated.

The women would plan their meals and shop together, then create their own individual masterpieces. They would drink numerous cups of tea "to keep them going," and they always burned their mouths tasting soups and stews that bubbled enticingly on the hot stove. The kitchen was always steamy, and it smelled divine—the aromas of baking bread, roasting chicken, and simmering cholent and goulash were always wafting through the air. Everyone talked about how the food should be prepared—and they often argued over whose recipe was the best. The most frequent argument was over whether or not to add sugar to a dish. Those of Polish origin (the Polacks) said no, but those with Lithuanian roots (the Litvaks) put a pinch of sugar in everything—"to bring out the flavor"!

The atmosphere was so focused on the delivery of the Friday night or festival meal that I never considered whether my female role models had lovely clothes, painted nails, or styled hair. These women from Poland, Russia, and Holland, with their grubby aprons (called *pinnys*), fingers stained red from peeling beets, and onion-tired eyes were my mentors. They are my heritage and the real source of my inspiration. They were true Yiddisher mamas, and I am proud to carry on their tradition with this book. I hope that it will provide you, the reader, an insight into the fascinating link between food and the celebration of Judaism.

Cooking and good food have been central to Jews since the time of the Bible. In fact, the Jewish religion places the kitchen as the center of Jewish life as much as it does the synagogue because of its role in promoting family values. The Jewish calendar is studded with a glorious variety of festivals and holidays. Some of them are serious occasions; others are more fun. But they all have one thing in common: a celebratory shared meal, with a signature dish chosen for its religious connection to the holiday.

But good food is not restricted to festivals. Every Friday night we welcome the arrival of the Sabbath, when families come together and celebrate the joy of life by eating the best food that they can afford.

There is no single Jewish cooking style. The Jewish culinary tradition encompasses a wide variety of cultures and cuisines. In order to gain insight into a Jewish mama's world, it's helpful to understand some of the history and traditions of her people.

Judaism is not only one of the oldest religions in the world, but it is also one of the most geographically widespread. Over the last 5,000 years, Jews have traveled to every corner of the globe—sometimes out of choice, other times under pressure or hardship. Wherever they have settled, Jews have incorporated many of the local dishes into their own culinary lives, adapting them to suit Jewish dietary laws. These laws, which are called kashruth, dictate the kinds of meat, poultry, and fish that may be eaten and the way in which fish and animals must be killed and prepared. Great care is taken to ensure that processed foods do not contain any forbidden products (such as shellfish and pork), and dishes are not allowed to contain both milk and meat. Jews who observe the kashruth have separate utensils, crockery, and cutlery that they use in the preparation of meat and in the preparation of recipes that include milk.

Most Jews living in Western Europe originated from Poland, Russia, and the Baltic. These so-called Ashkenazi Jews brought with them a culinary heritage of traditional foods such as soups, stews, stuffed vegetables, and hearty, starchy, sugary, comfort foods that served them well during the long, cold winter months of Eastern Europe.

The other main grouping of Jews are called Sephardi Jews. They originated from Spain and North Africa, and they settled around the Mediterranean and the Middle East. Their food traditions reflect the lighter, spicier foods, such as kebabs, rice, and salads, that are eaten in warmer climates.

When the State of Israel was founded as the Jewish homeland in 1948, both Ashkenazi and Sephardi Jews rapidly settled the area. As a result, a new Israeli Jewish cuisine developed. This cuisine featured the best of both "original worlds." Its tasty, satisfying dishes have been heavily influenced by scores of other cultures, but they feature the finest fresh local produce, and they are made following the ancient dietary laws. From falafel and hummus to goulash with savory rice, Israeli Jewish cooking is a fantastic "melting pot" of cuisines.

Because "traditional Jewish cooking" means different things to Ashkenazi, Sephardi, and Israeli Jews, the challenge in writing a book that deals with traditional Jewish recipes is to decide which "tradition" to follow, or to strike a balance among the three cuisines. In this book I have attempted to capture the geographic and ethnic cultures that have strongly influenced the many different varieties of Jewish cooking.

Welcome to my kitchen—come inside, and let's cook!

chapter one
APPETIZERS

Eggplant Dip

This is a tasty, versatile Sephardi dip that is usually served with a selection of crudités, sliced pita, or matzah crackers. It has a wonderful texture and flavor, and even those who aren't usually fond of eggplant often find this absolutely delicious. You can make this dish either on a gas stove, outdoor grill, or broiler.

PAREVE: contains no meat or dairy products / Passover-friendly / can be made in advance
PREPARATION TIME: 10 minutes / **COOKING TIME:** 15 minutes / **SERVES:** 6

2 regular eggplants (about 2 pounds total) ◆ 2 large garlic cloves, peeled and sliced thinly
1 tablespoon mayonnaise ◆ 2 teaspoons fresh lemon juice ◆ Salt ◆ Freshly ground black pepper
¼ cup pine nuts, for garnish ◆ 2 tablespoons coarsely chopped Italian parsley, for garnish

◆

1 Cut several 2-inch-long, 1-inch-deep slits in each eggplant. Push the garlic slices into the slits.

2 If using a gas burner, place the eggplant directly on the burner over a medium-high gas flame and roast, turning occasionally until soft (about 15 minutes). If using an outdoor grill, place the eggplant on the hot grill and roast, turning occasionally until soft (about 10 minutes). Remove from the heat and set aside to cool.

3 Remove and discard the skin from the eggplant. Place the eggplant in a large bowl and mash with a fork. Mix in the mayonnaise and lemon juice. Add salt and pepper to taste. Refrigerate covered until chilled.

4 Just before serving, place the pine nuts in a small, dry saucepan over medium-low heat. Toast, stirring frequently until golden brown (3 to 4 minutes). Sprinkle the pine nuts and parsley on the dip and serve.

Chopped Herring

Chopped herring is a much-loved, traditional appetizer in American Jewish households. It is most commonly eaten on slices of Challah (see pages 41 to 42) to break the fast at the end of Yom Kippur. This recipe is my mother's. Even with food processors and the kitchen accessories readily available today, my mother believes that the proper way to make this dish is to chop it by hand, using a large chopping cleaver.

PAREVE: contains no meat or dairy products / can be made in advance
PREPARATION TIME: 15 minutes / **COOKING TIME:** 0 minutes / **SERVES:** 4 to 6

One 24-ounce jar Bismark (pickled) herring, drained
2 tablespoons chopped onion from herring marinade
1 medium green or red apple, peeled, cored, and grated
2 slices challah or white bread ◆ 2 large eggs, hard-boiled and peeled

◆

1 Remove and discard the skins of the herring. Place the herring, onion, and apple on a chopping board and put aside.

2 Briefly dip the bread in warm water. Squeeze dry and place on the chopping board. Chop together with the herring, onion, and apple.

3 Remove and set aside the yolk of one egg. Add the egg white and remaining whole egg to the mixture and chop together to produce a pâté. Transfer the mixture to a serving dish.

4 Grate the reserved egg yolk. Sprinkle on top of the chopped herring and serve.

Falafel

Although the number of ingredients in this recipe may seem daunting, it's quite easy to make these deep-fried chickpea balls, and the taste of homemade falafel is simply without peer. This is the most popular street snack in Israel, and it's sold, wrapped in a pita, in kiosks, markets, and traditional restaurants. Israelis take their falafel very seriously—every year there are competitions to find the champion falafel maker, and there is fierce rivalry between street vendors and chefs. When it comes to falafel, fresh is definitely best; have your guests ready and waiting as the fritters come straight out of the fryer and onto their plates.

PAREVE: contains no meat or dairy products / can be made in advance / can be frozen up to 1 month
PREPARATION TIME: 30 minutes (plus at least 6 hours to allow chickpeas to soak)
COOKING TIME: 55 minutes / **MAKES:** about 40 fritters

1½ cups dried chickpeas ♦ 3 to 4 tablespoons bulgur ♦ 5 large garlic cloves, peeled
1 large yellow onion, peeled and chopped coarsely ♦ 5 tablespoons fresh Italian parsley
5 tablespoons fresh cilantro leaves ♦ 3 tablespoons ground cumin ♦ 1 teaspoon curry powder
1 tablespoon ground dried coriander ♦ 1 teaspoon baking powder
1 teaspoon cayenne pepper ♦ Freshly ground black pepper ♦ 1 large egg, lightly beaten
1 teaspoon salt ♦ ½ cup water ♦ 3 to 4 tablespoons graham flour ♦ About 6 cups vegetable oil

1 Place the chickpeas in a medium saucepan and cover with water. Let soak at least 6 hours or overnight.

2 Drain and rinse the chickpeas. Rinse the pan. Return the chickpeas to the pan, cover with water, and bring to a boil over medium-high heat. Reduce the heat to medium-low and simmer 45 minutes or until tender (add more water during cooking, if necessary). Drain.

3 Transfer the chickpeas to a food processor and pulse to a paste. Then empty into a large bowl. Stir in the bulgur and set aside.

4 Place the onion, garlic, parsley, cilantro, cumin, coriander, baking powder, salt, cayenne pepper, and curry powder in a food processor. Add pepper to taste. Process to a paste. Add to the chickpeas.

5 Add the egg and water to the chickpeas. Stir in the flour. If necessary, stir in a bit more water to prevent the mixture from being too dry or too thick. The consistency should be smooth and not too sticky.

6 Using wet hands, shape the mixture into small balls ready for frying.

7 Pour oil in a large, deep skillet to form a 2½-inch-deep layer of oil (or use a deep-fat fryer). Heat the oil over medium-high heat.

8 When the oil is very hot, place several balls into the oil (do not overcrowd the skillet) and cook until golden brown (3 to 4 minutes).

9 Using a slotted spoon, transfer the cooked balls to paper towels to blot any excess oil. Repeat until all balls have been fried. Serve immediately.

Knishes

These stuffed pastries are an American Jewish snack, but they are now also becoming popular with non-Jews from all ethnic groups. The knishes that are sold by street vendors in New York City and other large cities are often quite good—but homemade knishes are, of course, even better.

PAREVE: contains no meat or dairy products / can be made in advance / can be frozen up to 1 month
PREPARATION TIME: 40 minutes (plus 1 hour to allow dough to rest) / **COOKING TIME:** 45 minutes
MAKES: about 45 slices

DOUGH

1 cup all-purpose flour ◆ 1 teaspoon baking powder ◆ 2 large eggs ◆ 2 teaspoons kosher salt
3 tablespoons vegetable oil, divided ◆ 2 to 3 tablespoons cold water

FILLING

3 tablespoons vegetable oil ◆ 2 yellow onions, peeled and chopped finely
2 cups mashed potatoes ◆ Salt ◆ Freshly ground black pepper

GLAZE

Yolks of 2 large eggs, lightly beaten

◆

Mama says...
Be sure to very generously salt and pepper the potato filling to ensure a tasty knish.

1 Make the dough. Place the flour, baking powder, eggs, salt, 2 tablespoons oil, and 2 tablespoons water in a food processor that has been fitted with a dough blade and process until a smooth dough is formed. (If necessary, add 1 additional tablespoon water.)

2 Using the remaining tablespoon of oil, grease a large bowl. Place the dough in the bowl and let stand for 1 hour, covered.

3 Meanwhile, make the filling. Heat the oil in a medium saucepan over medium-low heat. Add the onions and sauté until golden brown (about 15 minutes).

4 Transfer the onions to a food processor that has been fitted with a metal blade. Pulse briefly to finely chop the onions.

5 Place the onions and potatoes in a medium bowl. Salt and pepper to taste, and mix well. Set aside until the dough has rested 1 hour.

6 Assemble the pastries. First, preheat the oven to 400°F.

7 Divide the dough into thirds.

8 Lightly dust a work surface with flour. Place 1 portion of dough on the work surface. Using a hand roller, roll the dough into a 20-inch by 8-inch strip.

9 Place one-third of the potato filling along the length of the strip. Cover the entire width of the strip. Starting at one end of the strip, roll up the strip to form a shape that resembles a jelly roll.

10 Repeat steps 8 and 9 with the remaining two portions of dough.

11 Place the pastries on a baking tray and glaze with egg yolk. Bake 30 minutes.

12 Cut into 1-inch-thick slices and serve immediately.

Hummus

This creamy chickpea purée is a specialty of Middle Eastern Jews, but it has become popular among non-Jews all over the world as well. Although it can be added to sandwiches, it is usually eaten with a hot pita as an appetizer. Traditionally, hummus is made with dried chickpeas, but canned chickpeas work nicely, too—and they make for a much faster preparation time. Tahini, a thick sesame seed paste, can be found in the ethnic section of most supermarkets. Be sure to thoroughly stir the tahini, which will have separated in its can or jar, before using.

PAREVE: contains no meat or dairy products / can be made in advance
PREPARATION TIME: 10 minutes / **COOKING TIME:** 0 minutes / **MAKES:** about 4 cups

Two 14-ounce cans chickpeas, drained and rinsed ◆ Juice of 1 lemon
3 tablespoons tahini paste ◆ ¼ cup, plus 2 tablespoons extra-virgin olive oil
3 garlic cloves, peeled and crushed ◆ Salt ◆ Cayenne pepper

◆

1 Place the chickpeas and lemon juice in a blender and purée. Add the tahini, olive oil, and garlic. Salt and pepper to taste. Blend until smooth.

2 Adjust the seasonings, if desired. Spoon into a serving dish and serve.

Mama says...
sprinkle with chopped parsley and olives, drizzle with extra-virgin olive oil, and serve with a hot pita.

Egg and Onion

*This is a simple, traditional dish that is often served alongside chopped liver
(see opposite) on Friday nights. It can be made with raw or cooked onion, and it is
delicious on rye bread, Challah (see pages 41 to 42), or matzah crackers.
For a mild onion taste, use cooked white onions. For a stronger onion flavor,
use raw or cooked yellow onions.*

FLEISHIK: contains no meat *or* **MILCHIK**: contains dairy products *or*
PAREVE: contains no meat or dairy products / Passover-friendly / can be made in advance
PREPARATION TIME: 10 minutes / **COOKING TIME**: 20 minutes / **SERVES**: 6

1 tablespoon chicken fat, margarine (nondairy for a meat meal), or vegetable oil
1 large yellow or white onion, peeled and chopped coarsely
8 large eggs, hard-boiled, peeled, and chopped finely
Salt ◆ Spanish paprika for garnish (if desired)

◆

1 Heat the chicken fat, margarine, or vegetable oil in a medium frying pan over medium-low heat.

2 If a light onion flavor is desired, place onion in the pan and sauté until soft and slightly browned. Remove from the heat and set aside.

(If a stronger onion flavor is desired, do not cook the onion.)

3 Finely chop or grate the eggs. Mix with the onions and salt to taste. Transfer to a serving bowl and sprinkle with paprika. Serve at room temperature.

Grandma's Chopped Liver

My mother and grandmother have always made their own chopped liver for the family to enjoy on Friday nights. In fact, Friday nights wouldn't be the same without this delicacy, which is served with large, soft slices of challah (see pages 41 to 42) or matzah crackers. Although many people purchase chopped liver at their local deli, you can control the ingredients, freshness, and flavor, and serve a treat that any deli would be proud to sell by making your own (which is really easy to do).

FLEISHIK: contains meat / Passover-friendly / can be made in advance / can be frozen up to 2 weeks
PREPARATION TIME: 15 minutes / **COOKING TIME:** 10 minutes / **SERVES:** 4 to 6

2 to 3 tablespoons sunflower oil ◆ 2 large yellow onions, peeled and sliced thinly
9 ounces koshered chicken livers ◆ 3 large eggs, hard-boiled and peeled
Salt ◆ Freshly ground black pepper

◆

1 Heat the sunflower oil in a frying pan over medium-low heat. Add the onions and sauté until slightly browned (about 10 minutes). Add the chicken livers. Stirring occasionally, fry 5 minutes. Transfer the chicken livers and onions to paper towels to blot any excess oil.

2 Remove the egg yolk from one egg and set aside. Coarsely chop the egg white and remaining two eggs.

3 Place the chicken livers and onions on the work surface with the chopped eggs. Mince together. Transfer the mixture to a medium-sized bowl and mix well. Salt and pepper to taste. Refrigerate covered until ready to serve.

4 Just before serving, spread the mixture over crackers or place in a serving bowl. Grate or mince the remaining egg yolk. Sprinkle the egg yolk over the chopped liver and serve.

Tabbouleh

This satisfying tabbouleh is traditionally served with a selection of other salads and dips as part of an appetizer table, or as a side dish with meat or chicken. The members of my synagogue in North London have regular Friday night meals together where tabbouleh is often served with teriyaki salmon and fish balls. Serve this at room temperature to bring out the full flavor of the onions and tomatoes.

PAREVE: contains no meat or dairy products / can be made in advance
PREPARATION TIME: 15 minutes / **COOKING TIME:** 15 minutes / **SERVES:** 6

**2 cups bulgur ◆ 1 cup boiling water ◆ 10 plum tomatoes
5 scallions, chopped coarsely ◆ 6 tablespoons coarsely chopped fresh mint
3 tablespoons coarsely chopped Italian parsley
3 tablespoons extra-virgin olive oil ◆ Juice of 1 lemon
Salt ◆ Freshly ground black pepper**

◆

1 Place the bulgur and water in a medium saucepan. Bring to a boil over medium-high heat. Reduce the heat to low and simmer uncovered until the bulgur is tender (about 15 minutes). Transfer to a colander and drain off any remaining water. Set aside.

2 Fill a large saucepan with water and bring to a boil over high heat. Place the tomatoes in water and cook 2 to 3 minutes. Remove the tomatoes from the water. Peel off and discard the skins. Remove and discard the seeds. Coarsely chop the tomato flesh.

3 Transfer the bulgur to a serving bowl. Add the tomatoes, scallions, mint, parsley, olive oil, and lemon juice. Generously salt and pepper. Toss to mix.

*Mama says...
Scoop individual portions into small Bibb lettuce leaves. Top with chopped, pitted black olives and serve.*

Fried Eggplant Salad

I love to serve this salad as a first course for our Friday night meal when it's too hot for chicken soup. This is one of several Sephardi recipes given to me by a friend, who received the recipes from her Tunisian mother-in-law. It's a simple dish that uses few ingredients—but, as is the case with many recipes that have been handed down from generation to generation—the exact measurements of ingredients were never written down. This is the way I like to prepare it, but feel free to experiment with different measurements of your own, to suit your personal taste.

PAREVE: contains no meat or dairy products / Passover-friendly / can be made in advance
PREPARATION TIME: 10 minutes / **COOKING TIME:** 15 minutes / **SERVES:** 8

3 tablespoons olive oil
2 large eggplants, cut into bite-sized cubes (leave the skin on)
About 1 cup salty Israeli pickled cucumbers, chopped coarsely
1 bunch (about 1 ounce) Italian parsley, chopped coarsely ◆ Salt
Freshly ground black pepper

◆

1 Heat the olive oil in a large frying pan over medium heat. Add 1 layer of eggplant. Sauté until golden brown (about 5 minutes). Transfer to paper towels. Repeat until all the eggplant is fried.

2 Place the eggplant, cucumber, and parsley in a large bowl. Add salt and pepper to taste. Toss to mix. Transfer to a serving bowl or to individual salad plates.

Mama says...
Serve this tempting salad in a glass dish, garnished with thin slices of lemon.

Herring Salad

In the old days, herring made a regular appearance at Ashkenazi Eastern European dinner tables, as they were economical and tasty, and they kept forever when soaked in brine. Today a wide variety of prepared herring can be found in delis and supermarkets. The fish is always the same—the variety is in the marinade, which may be sweet, salty, spicy, garlicky, peppery, or lemony. Herring is not a personal favorite of mine, but I've found it to be surprisingly good when combined with beets, as in this salad. This recipe is quick and easy—and, because it requires no cooking, it's a pleasure to make during hot summer months.

MILCHIK: contains dairy products
PREPARATION TIME: 5 minutes plus 15 minutes to refrigerate / **COOKING TIME:** 0 minutes
SERVES: 6 to 8

2 medium golden delicious apples, cored, peeled, and chopped coarsely
20 ounces schmaltz herring, chopped coarsely
2 tablespoons pickled Israeli cucumbers, chopped coarsely
1 tablespoon sugar ◆ 2 teaspoons cider vinegar ◆ 1¼ cups sour cream
1 cup cooked beets, peeled and chopped coarsely

1 In a large bowl, combine the apples, herring, cucumbers, sugar, and cider vinegar. Add the sour cream and mix well. Stir in the beets. Refrigerate until chilled (about 15 minutes) and serve.

Mama says...
Serve this colorful salad in a glass bowl, and garnish it with fresh chives.

Chapter two

SOUPS, DUMPLINGS & BREAD

Borscht

The popularity of borscht throughout the centuries is no doubt related to the availability and cost of its main ingredient—the gloriously purple beet. In the twenty-first century, however, many enjoy it for another reason as well—it is low in fat and high in nutrients. My recipe is based on my great-aunt's. My great-uncle was from Russia, and he and my great-aunt made this every Passover. It was not an easy dish to make back then, as cooked beets were not available in stores during those days. Fortunately, they are available to us today. Borscht may be served hot or cold, chunky or smooth. Traditionally, it's served cold during the summer, with a dollop of sour cream, and hot in the winter, with a garnish of sliced boiled potato. Either way, its vibrant color and flavor will be sure to please. Beware of serving it at a table dressed in a white tablecloth, however!

PAREVE: contains no meat or dairy products *or* **MILCHIK:** contains dairy products *or* **FLEISHIK:** contains meat / Passover-friendly / can be made in advance
PREPARATION TIME: 15 minutes / **COOKING TIME:** 40 minutes / **SERVES:** 4

4 cups water ◆ 1 teaspoon kosher salt ◆ 2 large eggs ◆ Juice of 1 lemon
One 2-pound cooked beet (about a 3-inch diameter), peeled and chopped coarsely
3 tablespoons light brown sugar to taste

◆

1 Place the water in a large saucepan. Stir in the salt. Add the chopped beet.

2 Bring to a boil over medium-high heat. Reduce the heat to medium-low and simmer for 30 minutes.

3 In a small bowl, whisk together the eggs, lemon juice, and sugar. Add to the soup. Cook, stirring constantly, for 3 minutes.

4 Transfer half of the soup to a food processor. Process until the mixture is smooth. Return the mixture to the saucepan. Serve warm or chilled.

Thick Cabbage and Bean Soup

The original cabbage soup that was made in Eastern Europe was probably created as a way to use up overripe vegetables. Today, many Jewish mamas add cannellini beans for extra nutrition. Hearty and flavorful, with a delightful combination of colors, textures, and tastes, this is the perfect soup to serve on cold winter days.

PAREVE: contains no meat or dairy products / can be made in advance / can be frozen up to 2 weeks
PREPARATION TIME: 25 minutes / **COOKING TIME:** 40 minutes / **SERVES:** 6

**2 tablespoons olive oil ◆ 1 medium yellow onion, peeled and chopped finely
3 medium carrots, peeled and chopped coarsely ◆ 2 medium potatoes,
peeled and chopped coarsely ◆ 2 medium zucchini, trimmed and chopped coarsely
3 large garlic cloves, peeled and chopped finely ◆ 4 cups vegetable stock
4 cups coarsely chopped green cabbage ◆ 2 cups drained canned cannellini beans
Salt ◆ Freshly ground black pepper**

◆

1 Heat the olive oil in a large saucepan over medium-low heat. Add the onion, carrots, potatoes, zucchini, and garlic. Sauté 10 minutes.

2 Add the vegetable stock, cabbage, and cannellini beans. Generously salt and pepper.

3 Increase the heat to medium-high and bring to a boil. Reduce the heat to low and simmer 40 minutes or until all the vegetables are soft. Adjust the seasonings, if necessary.

4 Serve immediately.

Mama says...
Ladle the soup into deep bowls. Drizzle with swirls of extra-virgin olive oil and serve.

Golden Vegetable Soup

A familiar dish from the shtetls of Eastern Europe, this soup is packed with the goodness of winter root vegetables. I remember my mother serving this to me when I was little. Today, my children enjoy it. The garnish of toasted cashews is a modern touch that enhances both its flavor and appearance. To hide the ingredients from children who refuse to eat vegetables, I make a "no bits" version, which is blended into a completely smooth soup.

PAREVE: contains no meat or dairy products / Passover-friendly
can be made in advance / can be frozen up to 1 month
PREPARATION TIME: 20 minutes / **COOKING TIME:** 30 minutes / **SERVES:** 6

1 cup coarsely chopped cashews, crushed ◆ 2 tablespoons olive oil
2 onions, peeled and sliced ◆ 1 medium rutabaga, peeled and chopped coarsely
2 medium potatoes, peeled and chopped coarsely
8 medium carrots, peeled and sliced into rounds ◆ 5 cups vegetable stock
Fine sea salt ◆ Freshly ground black pepper

◆

1 Preheat the oven to 400°F.

2 Place the crushed cashews on a baking tray and toast in the oven 8 to 10 minutes. Remove from the oven and put to one side to garnish the soup later.

3 Heat the olive oil in a large, deep saucepan over medium-low heat. Add the onions and sauté 2 minutes.

4 Add the rutabaga, potatoes, carrots, and vegetable stock and bring to a boil. Simmer until the vegetables are soft (about 20 minutes).

5 Transfer 4 ladles of vegetables and broth to a blender and blend until smooth. Return to the saucepan, stir to mix, and salt and pepper to taste.

6 Pour the soup into individual bowls. Garnish with toasted cashews and serve immediately.

Split Pea Soup

A large number of recipes were invented during World War II, when Eastern European Jews sought to maintain their health and put meals on the table in spite of the lack of fresh food available. These recipes often incorporate dried foods of some sort. This is one such recipe—it features nutritious legumes.

FLEISHIK: contains meat / can be made in advance / can be frozen up to 1 month
PREPARATION TIME: 15 minutes (plus 12 or more hours to allow legumes to soak)
COOKING TIME: 70 minutes / **SERVES:** 6

**1 cup dried yellow split peas, rinsed ◆ 2 medium celery stalks with leaves
2 tablespoons vegetable oil ◆ 2 medium yellow onions, peeled and chopped coarsely
1 medium carrot, peeled and chopped coarsely ◆ 6¼ cups beef stock
Salt ◆ Freshly ground black pepper**

◆

1 Place the peas in a large saucepan. Cover with cold water and let sit a minimum of 12 hours.

2 Drain and rinse the peas. Rinse the saucepan. Return the peas to the saucepan, cover with cold water, and bring to a boil over medium-high heat. Reduce the heat to low and simmer 40 minutes. Drain and rinse the peas, and set aside.

3 Trim the celery. Coarsely chop the leaves and set aside. Coarsely chop the celery stalks.

4 Heat the vegetable oil in a large saucepan over medium-low heat. Add the onions, chopped celery stalks, and carrot, and sauté until soft (about 5 minutes).

5 Add the beef stock and peas to the vegetables. Increase the heat to medium-high and bring to a boil. Reduce heat to low and simmer 25 minutes.

6 Transfer the mixture to a food processor or a blender (in batches, if necessary). Blend until the mixture is smooth. Salt and pepper to taste.

7 Pour the soup into individual serving bowls. Garnish with the chopped celery leaves and serve immediately.

Hearty Lentil Soup

*This rustic winter soup was a real favorite of my mother's when she was a little girl.
I'm not sure that she was aware that lentils are naturally low in fat, high in fiber,
and rich in protein—she just loved the taste! I like to make this with red lentils, as
they give the soup a wonderful color, but green lentils can be used instead, if desired.*

PAREVE: contains no meat or dairy products / can be made in advance / can be frozen up to 1 month
PREPARATION TIME: 15 minutes / **COOKING TIME:** 45 minutes / **SERVES:** 6 to 8

**2 tablespoons vegetable oil ♦ 2 medium yellow onions, peeled and chopped coarsely
2 medium carrots, peeled and chopped coarsely ♦ 2 celery stalks, chopped finely
1 medium potato, peeled and chopped coarsely ♦ 7 cups hot vegetable stock
1½ cups dried red lentils, rinsed ♦ Two 14-ounce cans tomatoes chopped with juice ♦ Salt
Freshly ground black pepper ♦ 6 to 8 sprigs fresh Italian parsley, for garnish**

♦

1 Heat the vegetable oil in a large saucepan
over medium-low heat. Add the onions, carrots,
celery, and potato and sauté 5 minutes,
stirring occasionally.

2 Add the vegetable stock, lentils, and tomatoes.
Salt and pepper to taste.

3 Increase the heat to medium-high and bring to
a boil. Reduce the heat to low and simmer
40 minutes. Adjust seasonings, if necessary.

4 Transfer to large, individual soup bowls.
Garnish the bowls with parsley sprigs and
serve hot.

Barley Soup

This is a hearty soup that hails from the farming communities of Poland and the Baltic states. My grandmother loved to make this as an alternative to chicken soup. She considered it "the next best thing to 'Jewish penicillin,'" as it contains a nourishing combination of ingredients.

FLEISHIK: contains meat *or* **PAREVE:** contains no meat or dairy products
can be made in advance / can be frozen up to 1 month
PREPARATION TIME: 15 minutes / **COOKING TIME:** 1 hour / **SERVES:** 6 to 8

2 tablespoons nondairy margarine or vegetable oil (for a pareve dish)
2 medium yellow onions, peeled and chopped coarsely
3 medium turnips, peeled and chopped coarsely ◆ 1 leek, trimmed and chopped coarsely
1 cup sliced cremini mushrooms ◆ 7 cups vegetable stock
1 cup pearl barley ◆ ½ cup dry red wine (if desired) ◆ Salt
Freshly ground black pepper ◆ 6 to 8 sprigs fresh Italian parsley, for garnish

1 Heat nondairy margarine or vegetable oil in a large, deep saucepan over medium-low heat. Add the onions, turnips, leek, and mushrooms and sauté 5 minutes.

2 Add the vegetable stock, barley, and, if desired, wine. Generously salt and pepper. Bring to a boil and reduce to simmer 45 minutes.

3 Transfer 4 large ladles of the vegetables, barley, and broth to a food processor or a blender. Blend until smooth. Return to the saucepan and stir to mix.

4 Adjust the seasonings, if necessary. Pour into individual soup bowls, garnish with parsley sprigs, and serve hot.

Knaidlach or Matzah Balls

Although these soft Jewish dumplings add texture and flavor to any soup, they may be most "at home" in Chicken Soup (see next page). Knaidlach are light, fluffy dumplings made from fine-ground matzah meal. Matzah balls are somewhat heavier, and they are made from medium-ground matzah meal. A scarcity of either type of dumpling can cause family disputes, so always ensure that each person is served an equal number of these favorites, and have extras on hand for seconds. Serve these in soup, along with a bit of Challah (see pages 41 to 42), as a first course, or as a light lunch.

FLEISHIK: contains meat / Passover-friendly / can be made in advance
can be frozen, uncooked, up to 1 month
PREPARATION TIME: 25 minutes / **COOKING TIME:** 15 minutes / **MAKES:** about 30 small dumplings

1 cup matzah meal (medium-ground for matzah balls; fine-ground for knaidlach)
2 tablespoons ground almonds ♦ 2 tablespoons chicken fat or vegetable oil ♦ 1 large egg
Kosher salt ♦ Freshly ground black pepper ♦ 2 cups simmering soup

♦

1 In a medium bowl, mix together all the ingredients. Refrigerate 30 minutes.

2 With wet hands, shape the mixture into small balls. Refrigerate covered, or use immediately.

3 Gently drop the dumplings into simmering soup and cook uncovered for 15 minutes. If they have been frozen first, allow them to thaw for 15 minutes before using.

mama says...
Make the soup for these dumplings a day ahead of time and refrigerate it overnight. Its flavor will be even better, and you can use the schmaltz (fat) that rises to the top of the soup to make your knaidlach or matzah balls the next day.

Ultimate Chicken Soup

Chicken soup is an essential part of the traditional Friday night family meal in most Ashkenazi homes. We welcome in the Sabbath with a meal fit for royalty, and this soup's broth more than meets that standard. Jewish chicken soup is also known as "kosher penicillin," and any Jewish mama will attest to its magical healing properties. Perhaps it's the nutrients in the soup, or perhaps it's the soothing effect of breathing in its tantalizing steam. One thing is for certain, however: no other medicine tastes as good! Every Jewish mama has her own recipe for chicken soup, and every Jewish mama believes that hers is the best. I like to leave the skin on the onions to give extra color and flavor (they're strained out before the soup is served), and I cut the carrots into decorative shapes to encourage the children to eat their vegetables. The secret of any good soup is in its stock, so make sure to use the best that you can. The longer the soup cooks, the more flavorful it will be.

FLEISHIK: contains meat / Passover-friendly
must be made at least 1 day in advance / can be frozen up to 1 month
PREPARATION TIME: 20 minutes (plus at least 12 hours, to refrigerate)
COOKING TIME: 3 hours / **SERVES:** 12 to 14

½ boiling fowl ◆ 1 raw chicken carcass ◆ 1 package (about 8 ounces) chicken giblets
2 turkey necks (about 8 ounces total), cut into small pieces ◆ 28½ cups water
4 medium carrots, peeled and sliced thinly ◆ 5 celery stalks, sliced thinly
2 parsnips, peeled and cut into large slices
2 turnips, peeled and sliced thinly ◆ 1 rutabaga, peeled and sliced thinly
2 yellow onions, unpeeled, halved ◆ 2 small tomatoes, halved
4 tablespoons powdered chicken bouillon or 3 chicken bouillon cubes
2 tablespoons kosher salt ◆ 3 fresh or dried bay leaves ◆ 3 black whole peppercorns

◆

1 Divide the fowl into large pieces.

2 Place all the ingredients in a large stockpot. Bring to a boil over medium-high heat. Reduce the heat to low and simmer 3 hours, occasionally skimming off the fat from the surface of the mixture (the fat may be refrigerated up to 3 days for another recipe).

3 Remove from the heat and let cool to warm. Place a large strainer over a large saucepan.

Strain the soup mixture. Gently remove the vegetables that are still intact from the strainer and place in the broth. Remove the chicken meat and set aside for another meal. Discard all other ingredients in the strainer.

4 Refrigerate the soup uncovered for at least 12 hours.

5 When ready to serve, reheat the soup over medium heat. Serve piping hot.

Kreplach

*Kreplach are the Jewish equivalent of Italian ravioli or Chinese wontons.
These small, stuffed pasta packages are served in hot chicken soup, and they're
particularly popular during Rosh Hashanah and other festivals. Although they take
a little time to make, they are delicious. Once you've mastered the art of preparing
kreplach, I am sure that you will be making them regularly. If you have a pasta
machine gathering dust, now is the time to use it, as you will be able to make really
thin dough. (You can, of course, roll the dough out by hand, if you prefer.) Be careful
not to overfill the kreplach, and make sure they are well sealed before cooking.*

FLEISHIK: contains meat / can be made in advance
can be refrigerated (prior to boiling) up to 1 week or frozen (prior to boiling) up to 1 month
PREPARATION TIME: 45 minutes (plus 90 minutes to allow dough to rest)
COOKING TIME: 10 minutes / **SERVES:** 10 to 12 (**MAKES:** about 80 dumplings)

**2 cups all-purpose flour ◆ 2 large eggs ◆ 1 to 2 tablespoons kosher salt, divided
1 or more tablespoons cold water ◆ 1 tablespoon chicken fat or vegetable oil
1 small yellow onion, peeled and chopped very finely
½ cup ground cooked beef, chicken, or turkey ◆ Freshly ground black pepper
1 teaspoon finely chopped fresh flat-leaf parsley
Hot chicken soup (see pages 36 to 37; 1 cup per serving)**

◆

1 Make the pasta. Place the flour, eggs,
1 teaspoon kosher salt, and 1 tablespoon water
in a food processor fitted with a dough blade.
Mix, adding a bit more water if necessary, until
a smooth dough is formed (about 2 minutes).
Remove from the bowl and cover with plastic
wrap. Let sit 1 hour.

2 Meanwhile, make the filling. Melt the chicken
fat or vegetable oil in a medium saucepan over
medium-low heat. Add the onion and sauté until
soft (about 5 minutes). Add the beef, chicken, or
turkey and stir to mix.

3 Transfer the mixture to a food processor. Add the parsley, pepper, and 1 teaspoon salt and pulse to combine. Refrigerate until ready to use.

4 Divide the dough into six equal-sized portions. Using a pasta machine, roll one portion through the machine at each of its settings, until the dough has been rolled at the machine's thinnest setting. (If desired, the dough may be rolled out with a hand roller. Roll until the dough is paper thin.)

5 Using a 2-inch round cutter, cut out circles of the dough. Place ½ teaspoon of the meat filling in the center of each circle. Dampen the edges of each circle and fold over to make triangles. Dust some flour to prevent sticking. Repeat with the remaining portions of dough. Set aside 30 minutes before cooking.

6 Fill a large saucepan with water. Add 1 tablespoon salt and bring to a simmer over medium heat. Gently place the kreplach in simmering water and cook until the dumplings rise to the surface of the water and are just tender (about 5 minutes).

7 To serve, place the kreplach in individual bowls of hot chicken soup (6 to 8 kreplach per serving).

Challah

Challah is Jewish bread—it has been in our culture as long as there have been Jews. Details of its preparation are found in ancient religious texts and prayers, and its heritage goes back further than the time of the Great Temple in Jerusalem, where challah was given to the priests as an offering. Although today it is readily available in delis and most supermarkets, nothing beats the smell, taste, and satisfaction of homemade challah. I like to make mine with honey instead of sugar. The wonderful aroma that wafts from the oven indicates when the bread is done. Traditionally, challah is plaited (braided), and it's made of three, four, or six strands. At festival times (especially during Rosh Hashanah), however, challah is baked in round loaves. During the time from Rosh Hashanah to Simchat Torah, I add apples and raisins to the bread, as a symbol of the "sweet and fruitful" new year that we hope is to come. During Purim I glaze the bread with honey and sprinkle decorative cake sprinkles, and on Shavuot I form the dough into the shape of the Ten Commandments. This recipe calls for the challah to be made in three-strand plaits.

PAREVE: contains no meat or dairy products / can be made in advance / can be stored at room temperature up to 2 days, in the refrigerator up to 4 days, or in the freezer up to 2 weeks

PREPARATION TIME: 15 minutes (plus 2½ hours to allow dough to rise)

COOKING TIME: 35 minutes / **MAKES:** 2 large loaves

1 cup warm water, divided ◆ 1 tablespoon active dry yeast ◆ 1 teaspoon kosher salt

4¼ cups bread flour ◆ 1 tablespoon honey ◆ 2 large eggs

¼ cup, plus 1 tablespoon vegetable oil, divided

1 medium green or red apple, peeled, cored, and grated (if desired)

3 tablespoons dark raisins (if desired) ◆ 2 teaspoons cinnamon (if desired)

Yolks of 2 large eggs, lightly beaten ◆ 2 tablespoons poppy seeds

1 Place ½ cup warm water in a large bowl. Stir in the yeast and salt. Set aside until the mixture is foamy (about 10 minutes).

2 Place the flour, honey, 2 large eggs, and ¼ cup vegetable oil into a food processor. Process until the ingredients are well mixed. Add the yeast mixture. If desired, add the apple, raisins, and cinnamon.

3 While processing, gradually add the remaining water to form a smooth, springy dough that comes away from the sides of the bowl.

4 Using the remaining 1 tablespoon vegetable oil, grease a large bowl. Transfer the dough to the bowl and cover with plastic wrap. Set aside in a warm spot for 2 hours or until the dough has doubled in size.

5 Knock back the dough and divide in half. Divide each half into thirds. Roll each piece into a sausage shape.

6 Braid together 3 strands. Set aside. Repeat with the remaining 3 strands.

7 Cover the loaves with plastic wrap and set aside 30 minutes to allow the bread to rise again (this is called "proving").

8 Preheat the oven to 400°F.

9 Brush the egg yolks over the loaves. Sprinkle the loaves with poppy seeds. Place the loaves on a baking tray lined with nonstick baking paper. Bake 35 minutes or until golden brown. Bread should sound hollow when tapped on the bottoms.

Soup Croutons

Mandlen are bite-sized soup croutons that are exceptionally quick and simple to make and they are a great family favorite when served with tomato soup or Ultimate Chicken Soup (see pages 36 to 37). I was taught this particular recipe by my great-grandmother, who was brought up in Poland. It calls for the croutons to be deep-fried, but they can be baked instead, if preferred (see "Mama says"). For a modern twist, I sometimes add 1 teaspoon fresh, finely chopped basil or dried herbes de Provence to the mandlen dough.

PAREVE: contains no meat or dairy products / can be made in advance
can be stored in an airtight container up to 1 week
PREPARATION TIME: 10 minutes (plus 30 minutes to allow croutons to dry)
COOKING TIME: 10 minutes / **MAKES:** about 60 croutons

**1 tablespoon, plus about 3 cups vegetable oil, divided ◆ 1 large egg
1 teaspoon kosher salt ◆ ½ cup all-purpose flour**

1 Mix together 1 tablespoon vegetable oil, egg, and salt. Add the flour bit by bit, mixing until a dough is formed (some flour may not be used). Knead 10 minutes.

2 Lightly dust a work surface with flour. Using a hand roller, roll out the dough into a ¼-inch-thick sheet. Using a sharp knife, cut the pastry into ½-inch-wide diagonal strips. Reverse the direction and cut the pastry into ½-inch-wide diagonal strips to produce diamond-shaped croutons. Set aside for 30 minutes to dry.

3 Heat the oil in a deep-fat fryer.

4 Place the croutons in hot oil (in batches) and deep-fry until golden. Transfer to paper towels to remove any excess oil and let cool.

Mama says...
To bake croutons, preheat the oven to 400°F. Line a baking tray with parchment paper. Place the croutons on the tray and bake 10 minutes.

Homemade Bagels

There are as many stories about the origins and significance of bagels as there are different flavors of these breads themselves. The bagel—traditionally made as a humble, plain circle of bread—has now been adopted by America and most of the Western world as an incredibly popular snack food. Despite their almost universal acceptance today, bagels still have a significant role in Jewish life. They are traditionally eaten with hard-boiled eggs by mourners after a funeral, and they are also served to guests at circumcision ceremonies. The bagel's shape is said to symbolize the eternal cycle of life—hence its place at these occasions. Having no beginning or end, the bagel (the German word for "ring" or "bracelet") was long thought to protect from invasion by evil spirits, including the dreaded eyin hora (evil eye). This food of good fortune can, therefore, bring luck, blessings, and prosperity—as well as ward off demons!
Unlike most breads, bagels must be boiled before they are baked. This gives them their unique chewy and crispy texture and great fresh taste. Bagels go stale quickly, so if you have extras, cut them into thin slices and toast them for a great snack to enjoy at any time (except during Passover!).

PAREVE: contains no meat or dairy products / can be made in advance / can be frozen up to 1 month
PREPARATION TIME: 10 minutes (plus 2 to 2½ hours to allow dough to rise)
COOKING TIME: 30 minutes / **MAKES:** 12 bagels

1 cup warm water ◆ 1 tablespoon active dry yeast ◆ 1 tablespoon kosher salt
3 teaspoons sugar, divided ◆ 4½ cups bread flour ◆ 1 large egg, lightly beaten
3 tablespoons vegetable oil, divided ◆ White of 1 large egg
1 tablespoon cool or lukewarm water
2 to 3 tablespoons poppy seeds or sesame seeds (if desired)

◆

1 Place warm water in a medium bowl. Stir in the yeast, salt, and 1 teaspoon sugar. Set aside 10 minutes or until mixture is frothy.

2 In a food processor, mix together the flour, beaten egg, 2 tablespoons vegetable oil, remaining sugar, and yeast mixture. Process until the mixture forms a smooth, spongy dough.

3 Grease a large bowl with the remaining tablespoon vegetable oil. Place the dough in the bowl and cover with plastic wrap. Let sit 60 to 90 minutes or until the dough has doubled in size.

4 Knock back the dough to its original size and knead until all the air is pressed out and the dough is smooth.

5 Dust a work surface with flour. Divide the dough into 12 pieces and roll each piece into 7-inch-long, ½-inch-thick "sausages." Shape each "sausage" into a circle and carefully press the ends together to seal.

6 Line a baking tray with parchment paper. Place the bagels on a tray, cover with a damp towel, and let sit 1 hour to prove (rise again).

7 Preheat the oven to 425°F.

8 Fill a deep saucepan with water. Bring to a boil over high heat. Reduce the heat to medium and place 4 bagels in the pan. Cook for 2 to 3 minutes, until the bagels rise to the surface of the water. Remove the bagels from the water and place on a baking tray. Repeat until all the bagels have been boiled.

9 In a small bowl, mix together the egg white and 1 tablespoon water. Brush each bagel with egg-white wash. If desired, sprinkle the bagels with poppy seeds or sesame seeds.

10 Bake for 20 minutes or until golden brown. Remove from oven and let cool to warm before slicing and serving.

Mama says...
Serve bagels with cream cheese, snipped chives, lox or smoked salmon, and a dusting of black pepper.

Chapter three
MAIN COURSES

Smoked Trout Salad

Jewish people have a great affinity for smoked fish of all kinds, and trout is no exception. Whether served as a pâté, as part of a sandwich, or as a main course with potatoes and vegetables, smoked trout is extremely versatile. Because it's now available already smoked, it's also become a quick and easy ingredient for preparing wonderful meals.

PAREVE: contains no meat or dairy products / can be made in advance
PREPARATION TIME: 15 minutes / **COOKING TIME:** 10 minutes / **SERVES:** 4

SALAD
2 cups fresh or frozen peas
2 cups (about 8 ounces) fresh asparagus tips, sliced in halves
2 tablespoons olive oil ◆ 2 zucchini, trimmed and sliced into thin circles
3 cups (about 8 ounces) mixed salad leaves ◆ 1 cup fresh blueberries or raspberries, rinsed
4 large fillets (about 2 pounds smoked trout), skinned and flaked

DRESSING
2 tablespoons mayonnaise ◆ 2 tablespoons extra-virgin olive oil
1 tablespoon sesame seed oil ◆ Salt ◆ Freshly ground black pepper

◆

1 Make the salad. Place the peas and asparagus tips in a medium saucepan and cover with water. Bring to a boil over medium-high heat. Boil 4 to 5 minutes. Drain. Rinse with cold water (to prevent further cooking and to retain the color of the vegetables).

2 Meanwhile, heat the sesame seed oil in a frying pan over medium heat. Add the zucchini and sauté, turning occasionally, until just tender (about 2 minutes). Set aside 10 minutes to cool.

3 Place the peas, asparagus, zucchini, salad leaves, and blueberries or raspberries in a large salad bowl. Add the trout and gently mix to combine.

4 Make the dressing. In a small bowl, whisk together the mayonnaise, olive oil, and sesame seed oil. Salt and pepper to taste.

5 Place the salad on individual serving plates. Whisk the dressing and drizzle over the salads. Serve immediately.

Halibut with Egg-Lemon Sauce

This is a prime example of a fish dish that tastes better cold or at room temperature than it does warm. It's an ideal Passover supper dish that does not include nuts or matzah meal and is popular with the older generation because of its ease on the digestive system. My mother sometimes makes this recipe using mackerel instead of halibut. It provides a nice change of flavor, and mackerel is less expensive.

PAREVE: contains no meat or dairy products / Passover-friendly / can be made in advance
PREPARATION TIME: 20 minutes / **COOKING TIME:** 25 minutes / **SERVES:** 4

**Four 6-ounce halibut steaks, boned ◆ 1 large yellow onion, peeled and sliced thinly
1 bay leaf ◆ Salt ◆ Freshly ground black pepper ◆ Juice of 2 lemons
2 large eggs, lightly beaten ◆ 1 tablespoon (or more, to taste) sugar
1 teaspoon cornstarch or (for Passover) potato flour ◆ Slices of lemon, for garnish
Sprigs of Italian parsley, for garnish**

◆

1 Place the fish in a saucepan that is large enough for all the fillets to lie flat. Cover with water. Add the onion and bay leaf. Salt and pepper to taste.

2 Bring to a boil over medium-high heat. Reduce the heat to low and simmer until the fish is white and firm to the touch (about 15 minutes).

3 Gently transfer the fish to a serving plate. Transfer 1 cup liquid from the pan to a medium saucepan on low heat. Add the lemon juice, eggs, and sugar to liquid. Salt and pepper to taste.

4 Transfer 1 tablespoon liquid to a small bowl or glass. Discard the remaining liquid.

5 Place the cornstarch or potato flour in a bowl or glass with liquid and whisk to blend. Pour into the lemon-juice sauce, whisking constantly.

6 Still over low heat, cook, stirring constantly, until the sauce coats the back of a spoon (about 3 minutes). Do not allow the sauce to come to a boil. Adjust the seasonings, if desired, and remove from the heat.

7 Pour the sauce over the fish. Chill or set aside until the dish has reached room temperature (about 30 minutes).

8 Serve with lemon slices and parsley sprigs.

Mother-in-Law's Boiled Gefilte Fish

My mother-in-law passed this popular recipe down to me. In the tradition of Jewish cuisine, cooks simply added a little of this and a bit of that until the right combination was achieved. My late husband encouraged me to undergo "fish ball training" with his mother as part of our engagement! The fish balls can be cooked in a deep-fat fryer or boiled in fish stock, which is the lighter of the two versions.

PAREVE: contains no meat or dairy products / Passover-friendly
can be made in advance / can be frozen up to 2 weeks
PREPARATION TIME: 20 minutes / **COOKING TIME:** 1 hour / **SERVES:** 10 to 12 (**MAKES:** 40 small balls)

FISH STOCK
4 cups water ◆ 4 yellow onions, peeled and sliced thinly
½ pound bones and skin of fish (any type) ◆ 2 celery stalks
2 medium carrots, peeled and sliced thinly ◆ 2 tablespoons parsley
2 teaspoons kosher salt ◆ 2 black whole peppercorns ◆ 2 bay leaves ◆ 1 to 2 tablespoons sugar

FISH BALL MIXTURE
1 pound boneless, skinless haddock ◆ 1 pound boneless, skinless cod ◆ 1 pound boneless, skinless bream ◆ 1 large yellow onion, peeled and chopped finely ◆ 2 large eggs
2 to 3 tablespoons medium-ground matzah meal ◆ 1 tablespoon vegetable oil ◆ 2 teaspoons kosher salt ◆ 1 teaspoon white pepper ◆ 2 teaspoons sugar ◆ 1 drop almond extract

◆

1 Make the fish stock. Place all the ingredients in a large saucepan. Bring to a boil over medium-high heat. Reduce heat and simmer 15 minutes.

2 Make the fish ball mixture. Mince the fish in a food processor. Add the remaining ingredients. Pulse until light and sticky. Season if necessary.

3 Make the fish balls. Using wet hands, roll fish mixture into egg-sized balls. Using the palm of your hand, flatten the balls slightly. Place balls in fish stock and cook over medium heat 45 minutes.

4 Using a slotted spoon, transfer the fish balls to a serving platter.

Fish Pie

Jewish people love fish. Even the Talmud discusses mystical values surrounding the tradition of eating fish on the Sabbath. This savory pie, made with flaked cooked fish and topped with mashed potatoes, is a delicious, warming dish to serve on cold winter evenings. I like to use a mixture of fresh and smoked haddock, but fresh and smoked cod or trout work just as well. To save time, ask your fish merchant to "pin bone" the fillets for you. Otherwise, use tweezers to remove the bones yourself.

MILCHIK: contains dairy products / can be made in advance / can be frozen up to 1 month
PREPARATION TIME: 40 minutes / COOKING TIME: 75 minutes / SERVES: 6

PIE FILLING
24 ounces fresh haddock fillets, skinned ◆ 24 ounces smoked haddock fillets, skinned
About 3 cups milk ◆ 1 tablespoon olive oil ◆ 1 tablespoon butter
1 yellow onion, peeled and chopped coarsely ◆ 1 tablespoon ground dried coriander
1 tablespoon all-purpose flour ◆ 1 teaspoon dry mustard (any variety) ◆ Salt
Freshly ground black pepper ◆ 3 large eggs, hard-boiled, peeled, and chopped coarsely
10 scallions (about 4 ounces total), chopped coarsely
2 to 3 tablespoons Italian parsley, chopped coarsely
(reserve 3 to 5 sprigs for garnish)

POTATO TOPPING
4 boiling potatoes, peeled and chopped coarsely ◆ 3 tablespoons milk
½ cup unsalted butter ◆ Salt ◆ Freshly ground black pepper

◆

1 Make the pie filling. Cut the fish into small bite-sized pieces. Place in a medium-sized saucepan. Cover with 2½ cups milk.

2 Bring to a boil over medium-high heat. Reduce the heat to medium-low and simmer 10 minutes.

3 Place a colander over a large bowl. Drain the fish and set aside. Transfer the liquid to a heatproof 2-cup measuring glass. Set aside.

4 Heat the olive oil in a frying pan over medium-low heat. Add the yellow onion and coriander. Sauté 2 minutes. Set aside.

5 Add enough remaining milk to the liquid in a measuring glass to make 2 cups total liquid. Set aside.

6 Melt the butter in a medium-sized saucepan over medium-low heat. Stir in the flour. Cook 1 minute, stirring constantly. Still stirring, slowly add the milk liquid. Cook, and keep stirring,

until the sauce has thickened and coats the back of a spoon (about 5 minutes). Stir in the mustard. Generously salt and pepper to taste.

7 Preheat the oven to 400°F.

8 Flake the fish. Place in a large bowl. Add the egg, sautéed onion, scallions, parsley, and sauce. Gently stir to mix. Transfer to an ovenware dish, approximately 12 inches by 6 inches, and set aside.

9 Make the potato topping. Place the potatoes in a large saucepan. Cover with water and bring to a boil. Cook until very soft (about 15 minutes). Drain. Transfer to a large bowl and, using a potato ricer or a fork, mash. Add the milk and butter. Salt and pepper to taste. Stir to mix.

10 Spread the mashed potatoes over the fish mixture. Bake 1 hour, until the potatoes are crispy and golden brown.

11 Garnish with parsley sprigs and serve.

Mediterranean Salmon

This is a very popular recipe at the cooking classes I teach, and it has become something of a "signature dish" for me. In fact, it has almost reached iconic status at my dinner parties! The wonderful combination of salmon—the most popular fish in Jewish cuisine—red bell peppers, rosemary, and other ingredients provides all the flavors of the Mediterranean on one plate. I like to serve this with shredded green cabbage and mashed potatoes, rice, or crusty bread to soak up the delicious juices. This dish works well with cubed lamb instead of salmon, as well.

PAREVE: contains no meat or dairy products / Passover-friendly / can be made in advance
PREPARATION TIME: 10 minutes / **COOKING TIME:** 15 minutes / **SERVES:** 6

2 tablespoons olive oil ◆ 4 large red onions, peeled and chopped coarsely
3 large garlic cloves, peeled and chopped coarsely
2 red bell peppers, cored, and chopped coarsely
2 tablespoons all-purpose flour or (for Passover) potato flour ◆ 1 cup vegetable stock
1 cup dry red wine ◆ 2 tablespoons fresh rosemary, stemmed
(reserve 3 to 5 sprigs for garnish) ◆ 1 cup pitted black olives
Six 5-ounce salmon fillets, skinned and cubed ◆ Salt ◆ Freshly ground black pepper

◆

1 Heat the olive oil in a large frying pan over medium-low heat. Add the onions, garlic, and bell peppers. Sauté 3 minutes, stirring occasionally.

2 Stir in the flour. Cook 2 minutes, stirring frequently. Stir in the vegetable stock, wine, rosemary, and olives. Increase the heat to medium-high and bring to a boil. Add the salmon. Add salt and pepper to taste. Reduce the heat to medium and cook covered until the salmon is completely cooked (5 minutes).

3 Transfer to a serving platter. Garnish with rosemary sprigs and serve.

Fried Fish

Introduced by Sephardi Jews in the 1600s, fried fish is probably one of the most well-known Jewish dishes, and it is still popular now. As it tastes better cold, it is frequently fried in the day on Friday, refrigerated overnight, and served as a main course during Shabbat. Steaks of cod, halibut, and haddock, or fillets of flounder and sole are perfect for frying. I like to lightly salt the fish and let it sit for 30 minutes before frying it. This eliminates excess water from the fish and keeps the coating crispy.

PAREVE: contains no meat or dairy products / Passover-friendly
can be made in advance / can be frozen up to 1 month
PREPARATION TIME: 15 minutes (plus 30 minutes to allow salt to draw out excess water)
COOKING TIME: 5 to 8 minutes / **SERVES:** 6

3 pounds cut white-flesh fish fillets or steaks ◆ 2 teaspoons salt
½ cup fine-ground matzah meal ◆ ½ cup medium-ground matzah meal ◆ Freshly ground pepper
3 tablespoons all-purpose flour ◆ 2 large eggs, lightly beaten ◆ About 5 to 6 cups vegetable oil

◆

1 Rinse the fish in cold water and sprinkle lightly with salt. Place in a colander and let sit to drain 30 minutes. Using paper towels, pat the fish dry.

2 Combine the matzah meals, salt, and pepper. Place the flour, eggs, and seasoned matzah meal in 3 dishes (one ingredient per dish). Lightly dredge the fish in flour. Shake off the excess flour. Dip the fish in egg, evenly coating it. Dip the fish in matzah meal.

3 Preheat the oven to 350°F. Place the vegetable oil in a deep-fat fryer or a large frying pan to make a 1-inch layer of oil.

4 Heat over medium heat until the vegetable oil is hot (or until a small piece of bread dropped into the oil fries to a crisp within 30 seconds).

5 Place several pieces of fish in the oil. Fry the fillets for 3 to 4 minutes; fry the steaks 5 to 6 minutes. Gently turn the fish. Fry until golden brown on the bottom side (about 3 to 5 minutes). Transfer to a baking dish and place in the oven to keep warm while the remaining fish is frying. Repeat, adding and heating more oil if necessary, until all the fish is fried.

Friday Night Roast Chicken

My children look forward to this when they come in from school on Friday evenings. Many Jewish people cherish the quality time of Friday nights spent with extended family. My mother cooks her roast chicken plain, with some onion beneath the chicken and a bit of salt and pepper on top, and she keeps the roasting bird covered under aluminum foil until the last 15 minutes of its cooking time. The foil is then removed, which allows the skin to become crispy. To make gravy, she simply adds a little chicken stock and some boiling water to the pan juices. This recipe is a variation of my mother's, and it has evolved partly because I have a healthy spread of fresh rosemary in my garden throughout the year. Adding red wine and water to the roasting pan keeps the chicken succulent and prevents the flesh from drying out. I frequently serve this with Mushroom Rice (see page 73), Roast Potatoes (see page 79), and a selection of seasonal vegetables.

FLEISHIK: contains meat / Passover-friendly
PREPARATION TIME: 15 minutes / **COOKING TIME:** 75 minutes / **SERVES:** 6

4- to 5-pound roasting chicken (giblets removed)
2 tablespoons fresh rosemary ◆ 1 lemon, sliced into thin wedges
3 large garlic cloves, peeled ◆ 2 yellow onions, peeled and chopped coarsely
1 cup dry red wine ◆ Salt ◆ Freshly ground black pepper

◆

1 Preheat oven to 400°F. Pull the skin from the breast of the chicken and slip some rosemary, lemon wedges, and garlic cloves under it. Place the rest of these ingredients in the chicken cavity.

2 Arrange the onion in a roasting pan. Pour the wine over the onions. Add enough water so the pan is three-quarters full.

3 Place the chicken breast-side down in the pan. Salt and pepper to taste. Cover the pan with aluminum foil.

4 Bake for 80 to 85 minutes. Remove from the oven and leave to rest for 10 to 15 minutes. Carve into portions, and transfer to a serving platter.

Pot Roast

*My aunt in New York makes pot roast every Friday night, in a special pot kept just
for this purpose. This dish is as important to her family as roast chicken is to mine.
I like to serve this with Roast Potatoes (see page 79). The red wine adds a wonderful
flavor to the dish and helps to tenderize the meat.*

FLEISHIK: contains meat / Passover-friendly / can be made in advance
PREPARATION TIME: 15 minutes / **COOKING TIME:** 2½ to 3 hours / **SERVES:** 6 to 8

**1 cup dry red wine ◆ 1 cup beef stock ◆ One 3- to 4-pound beef brisket
2 large yellow onions, peeled and sliced thinly ◆ 2 medium carrots, peeled and sliced thinly
4 celery stalks with leaves, cut in half ◆ 2 tablespoons fresh parsley
4 large garlic cloves, peeled and chopped finely ◆ 2 bay leaves ◆ 2 tablespoons cornstarch**

◆

1 Place the wine and beef stock in a large
saucepan or roasting pan. Add water until the pan
is half full. Bring to a boil over medium-high heat.

2 Add the beef, onions, carrots, celery, parsley,
garlic, and bay leaves. Bring back to a boil. Reduce
the heat to low, cover, and simmer until the beef
is cooked through and tender (2½ to 3 hours).
Transfer the meat to a plate and set aside.

3 Place a colander over a bowl. Discard any
excess fat from the surface of the pan juices, then
pour the juices into a colander. Discard the bay
leaves. Set aside the vegetables to serve with the
beef (or discard them).

4 Place 2 tablespoons of the juices in a small
heatproof glass. Add the cornstarch and blend
to make a paste. Return the remaining juices to
the pan and heat over medium heat, stirring
occasionally, until the sauce thickens (about
3 minutes). Over medium heat, gradually add
this to the stock, stirring from time to time
until it thickens.

5 Slice the beef. Gently place it in the sauce and
warm gently.

6 Transfer the beef to a serving platter.
Top with the sauce and serve immediately.

Chicken or Turkey Schnitzel

I don't do everything my mother does—but one thing we do share is this recipe, and we both make it every week! My daughter makes it as well (she adds powdered chicken stock to the matzah meal to enhance the flavor of the dish). I think it is one of those very special dishes that everyone likes. Just cut up the schnitzel for the children and tell them it's nuggets! If you have any leftovers, try slicing them thinly and serving them with a salad for lunch the next day.

FLEISHIK: contains meat / Passover-friendly / can be made in advance / can be frozen up to 2 weeks
PREPARATION TIME: 15 minutes / **COOKING TIME:** 15 minutes / **SERVES:** 6

6 chicken breasts or 6 thick slices of turkey breast ◆ 4 tablespoons flour
Salt ◆ Freshly ground black pepper ◆ 2 large eggs, lightly beaten
1 cup medium-ground matzah meal or bread crumbs
4 to 6 tablespoons vegetable oil

◆

1 Place each piece of meat between two pieces of plastic wrap or parchment paper. Using a kitchen mallet or a rolling pin, pound the meat until thin and flat. (Be careful not to tear the meat.)

2 Place the flour in a shallow bowl. Season with salt and pepper. Place the eggs in a separate shallow bowl. Place the matzah meal or bread crumbs in a separate shallow bowl.

3 Lightly dredge each schnitzel in the flour, then dip in the egg, then dip in the matzah meal or bread crumbs, coating the schnitzel evenly.

4 Heat the vegetable oil in a large frying pan over medium heat. Add the schnitzels in one layer (they may be cooked in batches). Sauté until cooked through and golden brown (about 5 minutes). Turn them once during cooking.

Sweet and Sour Meatballs

One of my earliest memories of my grandmother's kitchen is of standing on a stool and helping her roll meatballs for dinner. We sang together and I told her all my secrets. My own busy daughters still find the time to help me roll meatballs—one of the few food preparations that must be performed in the original way.

FLEISHIK: contains meat / Passover-friendly / can be made in advance / can be frozen up to 1 month
PREPARATION TIME: 25 minutes / COOKING TIME: 1 hour / SERVES: 6

MEATBALLS
2 pounds ground beef ◆ 1 medium yellow onion, peeled and grated ◆ 1 large egg
2 tablespoons tomato purée ◆ 2 tablespoons medium-ground matzah meal ◆ ½ teaspoon salt
Freshly ground black pepper ◆ 2 tablespoons coarsely chopped fresh parsley

SAUCE
2 cups passata tomato sauce (available at specialty food stores and some grocery stores)
or two 14-ounce cans of diced tomatoes with juice ◆ Juice of 1 medium lemon
¼ cup packed light brown sugar ◆ 1 bay leaf ◆ 1 to 2 tablespoons white or red wine vinegar
2 cups beef stock ◆ 1 tablespoon potato flour ◆ 2 tablespoons cold water ◆ Salt
Freshly ground black pepper ◆ Sprigs of basil, for garnish

◆

1 Make the meatballs. By hand or in a food processor, thoroughly combine all the ingredients. Shape the mixture into 2-inch balls.

2 Make the sauce. Place all the ingredients except the potato flour and water in a large saucepan. Bring to a boil over medium-high heat. Reduce the heat to medium-low and simmer 10 minutes.

3 Gently place the meatballs in sauce. Reduce the heat to low, cover the pan, and simmer 40 minutes.

4 In a small glass, mix potato flour and water to a paste. Stir into sauce. Increase heat to medium and cook until sauce is thick, stirring constantly.

5 Transfer meatballs to a deep serving dish. Top with sauce and garnish with basil. Serve with rice.

Beef Strudel

Meat loaves and strudels (meat loaves with pastry) have always been part of the Jewish mama's culinary repertoire, probably because they are economical and tasty, and because they can be made in different shapes and quantities. Best of all, perhaps—children will eat them! Although I call for beef here, strudels can be made with chicken, turkey, or lamb, as well. For a Passover-friendly dish, omit the pastry and simply serve this as a meat loaf.

FLEISHIK: contains meat / can be made in advance / can be frozen, uncooked, up to 2 weeks
PREPARATION TIME: 40 minutes / COOKING TIME: 1 hour / SERVES: 8

STRUDEL
2 tablespoons olive oil ◆ 1 medium yellow onion, peeled and chopped finely
3 large garlic cloves, peeled and chopped finely ◆ 1 tablespoon ground cumin
2 pounds beef, ground ◆ 2 tablespoons ketchup or tomato purée
2 tablespoons medium-ground matzah meal ◆ 1 large egg, lightly beaten
2 tablespoons fresh oregano, chopped coarsely ◆ 2 teaspoons salt
1 teaspoon freshly ground black pepper ◆ One 15 x 10 inch sheet (about 12½ ounces)
of thawed frozen puff pastry

GLAZE AND TOPPING
Yolk of 1 large egg ◆ 2 tablespoons raw sesame seeds

SAUCE
2 tablespoons olive oil ◆ 1 medium yellow onion, peeled and chopped finely
4 large garlic cloves, peeled and chopped finely ◆ 1 carrot, peeled and chopped finely
Two 14-ounce cans diced tomatoes with juice ◆ 1 tablespoon tomato purée
½ cup dry red wine ◆ 2 to 3 tablespoons fresh basil, chopped coarsely
(reserve 8 whole small basil leaves for garnish) ◆ 1 teaspoon sugar
Salt ◆ Freshly ground black pepper

1 Preheat the oven to 400°F.

2 Line a baking tray with baking parchment paper.

3 Make the strudel. Heat the olive oil in a medium frying pan over medium-low heat. Add the onion, garlic, and cumin and sauté until the onion is soft (about 5 minutes).

4 Place the onion mixture, beef, ketchup, matzah meal, egg, oregano, salt, and pepper in a food processor. Process until well blended. (Or, place the ingredients in a large bowl and mix by hand until well blended.)

5 Lightly flour a work surface. Place the pastry on the work surface and roll out until the sheet is about 14 inches by 9 inches (the pastry should be quite thin). Place the meat lengthwise along the center of the pastry, leaving a 1-inch border on all sides. Brush the edges of the pastry with a bit of water. Fold in the side edges and roll up. The pastry should resemble a jelly roll.

6 Place the pastry on the baking tray. Brush with the egg yolk and sprinkle with sesame seeds. Bake for 40 minutes or until the pastry is golden and crispy.

7 Meanwhile, make the sauce. Heat the olive oil in a medium saucepan over medium heat. Add the onion, garlic, and carrot and sauté 3 minutes. Add the tomatoes, tomato purée, wine, basil, and sugar. Salt and pepper to taste. Increase the heat to medium-high and bring to a boil.

8 Reduce the heat to low and simmer covered 40 minutes.

9 Transfer the sauce to a food processor and pulse briefly to make a smoother sauce. Return the sauce to the pan. Adjust seasonings, if necessary.

10 To serve, cut the strudel into thick slices and place on a serving platter or on individual serving plates. Top with the sauce, and garnish with the reserved basil leaves.

Mama says...
A good meat strudel is highly seasoned. Overdo it a bit with the seasonings, as the spices need to permeate through the pastry layer into the meat.

Goulash

This Hungarian meat stew was a great favorite of my family's when I was a child, and my mother used to prepare it whenever my grandmother came to visit. I have fond memories of my sisters and me—who were always starving after a long morning spent at Cheder (the Jewish equivalent of Sunday school)—running up the drive and being greeted with the wonderful aroma of this dish.

FLEISHIK: contains meat / can be made in advance / can be frozen up to 2 weeks
PREPARATION TIME: 30 minutes / **COOKING TIME:** 2 hours, 20 minutes / **SERVES:** 6 to 8

3 tablespoons vegetable oil ◆ 6 medium yellow onions, peeled and sliced thinly
2 medium red bell peppers, cored, seeds removed, and chopped coarsely
4 garlic cloves, peeled and chopped finely ◆ 1 to 2 tablespoons hot Hungarian paprika
4 pounds good-quality chuck steak, trimmed and cubed ◆ 2 tablespoons flour
2 cups dry red wine ◆ 2 cups beef stock ◆ Two 14-ounce cans diced tomatoes with juice
1 teaspoon sugar ◆ 1 tablespoon caraway seeds ◆ Salt
Freshly ground black pepper ◆ Sprigs parsley, for garnish

◆

1 Heat the vegetable oil in a deep, wide saucepan over medium heat. Add the onions, bell peppers, garlic, and paprika. Sauté 5 minutes. Transfer to a plate and set aside.

2 Using the same saucepan, sauté the meat until it has become brown on all sides (about 5 minutes). Return the onion mixture to the saucepan. Add the flour. Heat, stirring constantly, for 1 minute.

3 Stir in the wine, beef stock, tomatoes, sugar, and caraway seeds. Salt and pepper to taste. Then increase the heat to medium-high and bring to a boil. Reduce the heat to low and simmer covered, stirring occasionally, until the meat is cooked through and tender (about 2 hours). Adjust the seasonings, if desired.

4 Transfer the goulash to a serving platter. Garnish with parsley sprigs and serve.

Cholent

Cholent is one of the most familiar of all Jewish traditional dishes. It is a one-pot meal that features meat, grains, and vegetables, all cooked together for a very long time in very low heat and topped with delicious potato dumplings. In Jewish households, the cooking process starts on Friday, and the dish is normally served for lunch after the synagogue service on Shabbat. As it is prohibited to actually cook on Shabbat, this is the perfect way of providing a ready-to-eat hot meal. In the shtetls of Eastern Europe during the late nineteenth century, pots of cholent were cooked in communal bakers' ovens, which were large enough to generate and retain an incredible amount of heat. The families would go after synagogue to collect their pots of Cholent and partake of their Sabbath meal. One of the best things about Cholent is the incredible aroma it creates as it cooks.

FLEISHIK: contains meat / Must be made 1 day in advance
PREPARATION TIME: 40 minutes (plus 6 hours to allow beans to soak)
COOKING TIME: 18 to 20 hours / **SERVES:** 8

STEW

1⅓ cups navy or butter beans ◆ ¼ cup, plus 2 tablespoons olive oil ◆ 2 medium yellow onions, peeled and chopped coarsely ◆ 6 large garlic cloves, peeled and chopped coarsely
28 ounces beef brisket, cut into chunks ◆ ½ cup pearl barley
3 carrots, peeled and thinly sliced ◆ 3 baking potatoes, peeled and cut into large chunks
1 small turnip, peeled and chopped coarsely ◆ 1 celery stalk, chopped coarsely
One 14-ounce can chopped tomatoes with juice
4 cups beef stock ◆ 1 cup dry red wine ◆ 3 tablespoons corn syrup ◆ 8 large eggs
1½ tablespoons Hungarian paprika ◆ Salt ◆ Freshly ground black pepper

DUMPLINGS

2 boiling potatoes, peeled ◆ 1 medium yellow onion, peeled
2 tablespoons fine-ground matzah meal (or more, if necessary) ◆ Salt
Freshly ground black pepper

◆

Mama says...
The secret ingredient of my recipe for Cholent is the corn syrup, which softens and sweetens the other ingredients in a very subtle, unassuming way.

1 Place the beans in a medium saucepan. Cover with water. Let soak at least 6 hours.

2 Make the stew. Heat the olive oil in a large, deep, heavy-bottomed casserole over medium heat. Add the onions and garlic. Sauté 5 minutes.

3 Meanwhile, drain and rinse the beans.

4 Add the beef, beans, barley, carrots, potatoes, turnips, celery, tomatoes, beef stock, wine, corn syrup, eggs (in their shells), and paprika. Salt and pepper to taste. Add enough water so that all ingredients are covered with liquid.

5 Preheat the oven to 225°F.

6 Make the dumplings. Finely grate the potatoes. Finely grate the onion. Place the potatoes and onions between paper towels and squeeze to remove excess water.

7 Place the potatoes and onions in a large bowl. Add the remaining ingredients and mix well.

8 The mixture should be very firm; add more matzah meal, if necessary, to achieve this.

9 Shape the mixture into 2-inch balls and place on top of the stew mixture.

10 Bring the mixture to a boil over medium-high heat. Reduce the heat to very low.

11 Using aluminum foil, tightly cover the casserole. Place a casserole lid over the foil.

12 Bake 18 to 20 hours or overnight.

Mama says...
This stew may be cooked in a slow cooker, if you have one that's large enough. Use the lowest heat setting available.

Pickled Tongue or Salt Beef

Life for most people is so much easier today than it used to be in Eastern Europe. Nowadays, most kosher butchers sell prepared pickled ox tongue and brisket (or salt beef)—which is fortunate, because saltpeter, which is used in the pickling process, is no longer available to the public. To get the real "deli" pickled tongue or salt beef experience, just follow this recipe. Cook the meat slowly for a long period of time in order to get the most tender result possible. Use the meat as a filling for a chunky sandwich made with rye bread or pumpernickel, Coleslaw (see pages 82 to 83), and mustard, served on a platter with crispy french fries or Latkes (see page 131) and an assortment of pickles.

FLEISHIK: contains meat / Passover-friendly / must be made in advance / can be frozen up to 1 month
PREPARATION TIME: 10 minutes / **COOKING TIME:** 2½ to 3 hours / **SERVES:** 8 to 10

6 pounds pickled salt beef, pickled ox tongue, or brisket
2 medium red onions, peeled and halved ♦ 2 medium carrots, peeled and halved
2 bay leaves ♦ 1 tablespoon white wine vinegar ♦ 8 whole black peppercorns

1 Wash the meat thoroughly under cold running water. Put in a large saucepan and cover with cold water. Add the onions, carrots, bay leaves, white wine vinegar, and peppercorns.

2 Bring to a boil over medium-high heat. Reduce the heat to medium-low and simmer until tender (2½ to 3 hours), occasionally skimming the scum off the surface of the water. (Add more boiling water if necessary during cooking.)

3 Drain. Pour cold water over meat. Remove the skin and any gristle or excess fat from the tongue.

4 Wrap in aluminum foil and weigh down with a plate in the refrigerator. Slice the meat as desired.

Liver with Onions

This is a very tasty meal. I have to be in the right mood for it—liver does have its own flavor—but when I am, this is fantastic. The best side dish for this is mashed potatoes—flavor them with a spoonful of mustard and use them to soak up all those sweet onions. Delicious!

FLEISHIK: contains meat / Passover-friendly
PREPARATION TIME: 15 minutes / **COOKING TIME:** 20 minutes / **SERVES:** 6

**2 tablespoons olive oil ◆ 6 medium yellow onions, peeled and sliced thinly
1 tablespoon light brown sugar ◆ 2 tablespoons medium-ground matzah meal
Salt ◆ Freshly ground black pepper
3 pounds koshered chicken livers or 6 slices (about 3 pounds total) koshered ox liver
2 tablespoons vegetable oil ◆ ½ cup dry red wine**

◆

1 Heat the olive oil in a large frying pan over low heat. Add the onions and brown sugar. Cook 20 minutes, stirring occasionally, until the onions are golden brown and caramelized.

2 Place the matzah meal in a shallow dish. Add salt and pepper. Dust the liver with matzah meal.

3 In a separate frying pan, heat the vegetable oil over medium-low heat. Add the liver. Cook 3 to 4 minutes on each side. Pour the wine over the liver. Cook 2 minutes.

4 Arrange the onions on a serving platter. Top with the liver and serve immediately.

chapter four

SIDE DISHES

Chrain

Traditionally, horseradish is served on the seder plate at Passover to represent the bitterness of the Israelites when they were slaves in Egypt. Seder is the account of the exodus of Egypt led by Moses. It takes the form of a service at the dinner table and the seder plate includes symbolic foods to retell the story. Chrain is used throughout the year as a condiment—it livens up Gefilte Fish (see page 50), cold meats, and chicken. Be careful when grating horseradish, as the vapors it exudes are very powerful and can make you sneeze, cough, or cry (and that's before you've eaten it!). To temper the effect of this powerful ingredient, Jewish cooks mix it with beets, sugar, and vinegar to produce a wonderful relish called chrain. As Passover approaches, it is usually easy to find whole horseradish roots in supermarkets and Jewish delis. At other times of year, they are often only available at specialty food stores. Horseradish is quite easy to grow, however. My brother-in-law has a thriving crop in his backyard that it is always ready to pick just before Passover, when it is most needed.

PAREVE: contains no meat or dairy products / Passover-friendly / can be made in advance
PREPARATION TIME: 10 minutes / **COOKING TIME:** 0 minutes / **MAKES:** 2 cups

1 medium whole horseradish root (about 8 ounces)
3 medium beets (about 12 ounces total), boiled and peeled ◆ ⅔ cup white or cider vinegar
3 tablespoons light brown sugar or honey ◆ Freshly ground black pepper

◆

1 Open the kitchen window to help circulate air. Wearing rubber gloves, peel the horseradish.

2 Using a food processor or a hand grater, finely grate the horseradish. Place in a large bowl.

3 Finely grate the beets. Add to the horseradish. Add the vinegar and brown sugar or honey. Pepper to taste, and stir to mix.

4 Using boiling water, sterilize a 2-cup jar and its lid. Place the horseradish-beet mixture in the jar. Tightly seal. Refrigerate at least 2 hours before serving. Relish may be stored in the refrigerator up to 2 months. The pungency of horseradish varies considerably, so be sure to taste the relish and, if necessary, add a bit more brown sugar (or honey) or vinegar before placing it in the jar.

Mushroom Rice

This is one of my family's favorite dishes. I love to serve this with Roast Chicken on Friday nights (see page 57). I cook the rice in chicken stock to intensify the flavor. For a pareve dish, use vegetable stock instead.

FLEISHIK: contains meat *or* **PAREVE:** contains no meat or dairy products / can be made in advance
PREPARATION TIME: 10 minutes / **COOKING TIME:** 20 minutes / **SERVES:** 8 to 10

2 tablespoons extra-virgin olive oil ◆ 1 medium yellow onion, peeled and chopped coarsely
4 large garlic cloves, peeled and chopped finely
2 cups mixed fresh mushrooms, such as white, porcini, and wild mushrooms
5 cups chicken stock (fleishik), vegetable stock (pareve), or pareve chicken stock
2 cups long-grain white rice ◆ 1 tablespoon dried mushrooms
1 cup cooked, coarsely chopped asparagus (if desired) ◆ Salt
Freshly ground black pepper ◆ 2 tablespoons coarsely chopped fresh parsley

◆

1 Heat the olive oil in a large, deep-frying pan or saucepan over medium-low heat. Add the onions and garlic and sauté 3 minutes.

2 Add fresh mushrooms. Cook 5 minutes. (The mushrooms will release some juices; cook until the juices have been completely reabsorbed.) Set aside 2 tablespoons mushroom-onion mixture.

3 Add the chicken or vegetable stock, rice, and dried mushrooms to the pan. Increase the heat to

medium-high and bring to a boil. Reduce the heat to medium-low and simmer 10 minutes. Add the asparagus, if desired.

4 Turn off the heat, cover the pan, and let sit for 10 minutes.

5 Using a fork, fluff the rice. Salt and pepper to taste. Transfer to a serving bowl. Sprinkle with parsley and the reserved mushroom mixture. Serve immediately.

Potato Kugel

Kugels (savory casseroles) are a major feature of Ashkenazi cuisine, especially on Shabbat and during Yom Tov, when there are often extra guests to feed. Kugels freeze and reheat well, and they require little attention while cooking. Here I've taken my mother's recipe, made it healthier (by omitting egg yolks and calling for less oil), and added a stylish twist by making it in individual ramekins. If you prefer not to prepare individual servings, simply place the entire mixture in a shallow baking dish and bake for 45 minutes.

PAREVE: contains no meat or dairy products / Passover-friendly
can be made in advance / can be frozen up to 1 month
PREPARATION TIME: 20 minutes / **COOKING TIME:** 25 minutes / **SERVES:** 10

About 3 tablespoons olive oil ◆ 6 boiling potatoes, peeled
2 medium yellow onions, peeled and grated ◆ 4 tablespoons medium-ground matzah meal
1 tablespoon potato flour ◆ 1 teaspoon baking powder
Whites of 6 large eggs, lightly beaten ◆ 3 tablespoons extra-virgin olive oil
2 tablespoons fresh basil or parsley, chopped coarsely
1 teaspoon sugar ◆ Salt ◆ Freshly ground black pepper

◆

1 Preheat the oven to 400°F.

2 Line the base of 10 individual ramekins with nonstick baking paper. Lightly grease the sides of the ramekins with olive oil.

3 Using a food processor or a hand grater, grate the potatoes. Place the grated potatoes between paper towels and squeeze to remove any excess water.

4 Place the potatoes in a large bowl. Add the onions, matzah meal, potato flour, baking powder, sugar, egg whites, extra-virgin olive oil, and basil or parsley. Generously salt and pepper and mix well.

5 Spoon the mixture into the ramekins. Place in the oven and bake 25 minutes or until the tops are golden brown. Serve hot or chilled.

Pickled Vegetables

My friend Sharon, who is a Sephardi Jew, gave me this recipe, another favorite of mine. Pickled vegetables are generally served as a side dish to couscous in her community, but they are also delicious as part of an appetizer spread, as an edible served with cocktails, or simply as a snack. The process of pickling was created as a way to preserve vegetables, allowing them to be eaten out of season. The need to preserve vegetables in this way is no longer pressing, but pickling still lends enormous flavor and bite to most vegetables, and makes them a tasty addition to most meals. All kinds of vegetables—from turnips and beets to cauliflower and zucchini—may be pickled, and usually an assortment of such vegetables are served together. This recipe calls for one of my favorite combinations.

PAREVE: contains no meat or dairy products / Passover-friendly must be made at least 1 day in advance / **PREPARATION TIME:** 10 minutes (plus at least 12 hours to allow vegetables to pickle) / **COOKING TIME:** 0 minutes / **SERVES:** 6

**1 to 2 medium carrots, peeled and cut into short, fat sticks
1 orange bell pepper, cored and cut into short sticks
1 green bell pepper, cored and cut into short sticks ◆ 2 teaspoons salt ◆ 1 cup water
1 cup white wine vinegar (use kosher for Passover)**

1 Using boiling water, sterilize a clean 2-cup jar and its lid.

2 Sprinkle the vegetables with salt and place in the jar. Add water and vinegar. Tightly seal the jar with the lid and refrigerate at least 12 hours before serving. Use as desired.

3 Leave overnight in the refrigerator and use as desired.

Mama says...
These pickled vegetables may be stored in the refrigerator up to 2 weeks.

Ratatouille

This colorful combination of mixed vegetables is great with most main courses, and it can be served hot, warm, or cold. Even after refrigerating and reheating, this dish tastes fine and presents well.

PAREVE: contains no meat or dairy products / Passover-friendly / can be made in advance
PREPARATION TIME: 15 minutes / **COOKING TIME:** 15 minutes / **SERVES:** 6

3 tablespoons extra-virgin olive oil ◆ 2 medium red onions, peeled and chopped coarsely
1 large or 2 small eggplants (about 1½ pounds total), cut into bite-sized cubes (skin on)
2 medium zucchini, chopped coarsely
1 medium red bell pepper, cored and chopped coarsely
1 medium yellow bell pepper, cored and chopped coarsely
3 large garlic cloves, peeled and chopped finely
One 14-ounce can diced tomatoes with herbs
6 cherry or other small salad tomatoes, halved ◆ Salt
Freshly ground black pepper ◆ 4 tablespoons chopped fresh basil, divided

◆

1 Heat the olive oil in a large saucepan over medium heat. Add the onions and sauté 3 minutes.

2 Add the eggplant, zucchini, bell peppers, and garlic. Sauté 3 minutes.

3 Stir in the canned and fresh tomatoes. Salt and pepper to taste. Cook uncovered 10 minutes.

4 Stir in 2 tablespoons basil. Transfer the mixture to a serving platter and garnish with the remaining basil.

Potato Salad with Lemon Mayonnaise

This salad is also a regular at Shabbat lunches and, being pareve, it's served at Passover meals as well. It is healthy, economical, versatile, and delicious.

PAREVE: contains no meat or dairy products / Passover-friendly / can be made in advance
PREPARATION TIME: 10 minutes / **COOKING TIME:** 20 minutes / **SERVES:** 8

2 teaspoons sea salt ♦ About 20 baby new potatoes, cleaned and halved
Yolks of 2 large eggs ♦ Juice and zest of ½ medium organic lemon
1 teaspoon dry mustard (any variety) ♦ 1 tablespoon superfine sugar
Freshly ground black pepper ♦ 2 cups vegetable oil ♦ Snipped chives, for garnish

♦

1 Fill a large saucepan with water. Add 1 teaspoon salt. Bring to a boil over medium-high heat. Add the potatoes and cook until tender (about 20 minutes). Drain and set aside to cool.

2 Place the egg yolks, lemon juice and zest, mustard, and sugar in a blender or food processor. Salt and pepper to taste. Blend or process until the mixture is smooth.

3 With the blender running, slowly add the vegetable oil. Blend or process until the oil is thoroughly blended into the mixture. Adjust the seasonings, if desired.

4 Mix together the mayonnaise and cooled potatoes. Transfer to a serving bowl, garnish with chives, and serve.

Mama says...
To save curdled mayonnaise, gradually add one egg yolk while whisking the mayonnaise constantly.

Red Cabbage with Wine

This is delicious hot or cold, and makes a great side dish to almost any main course.

PAREVE: Passover-friendly / can be made in advance
PREPARATION TIME: 15 minutes / **COOKING TIME:** 30 minutes / **SERVES:** 6 to 8

**2 tablespoons extra-virgin olive oil ◆ 2 medium red onions, peeled and sliced thinly
8 cups red cabbage, shredded fine ◆ 1 cup kiddush or sweet red wine
1 cup white raisins ◆ 2 cups chicken stock (fleishik) or vegetable stock (pareve) ◆ Salt
Freshly ground black pepper ◆ 4 tablespoons nondairy margarine**

◆

1 Heat olive oil in a large saucepan over medium-low heat. Add the onions and sauté 5 minutes. Add the cabbage, wine, raisins, and chicken or vegetable stock. Salt and pepper to taste.

2 Increase the heat to medium-high and bring to a boil. Reduce heat to medium-low. Stir in the margarine. Simmer 30 minutes, stirring occasionally.

Crispy, Sliced Roast Potatoes

This is a very simple side dish that is delicious served with hearty main courses.

PAREVE: contains no meat or dairy products / Passover-friendly
PREPARATION TIME: 5 minutes / **COOKING TIME:** 30 minutes / **SERVES:** 6 to 8

8 large potatoes ◆ 2 tablespoons extra-virgin olive oil ◆ Salt

◆

1 Preheat the oven to 350°F. Cut the potatoes into 1-inch-thick slices. Rinse in cold water to remove excess starch. Blot dry with paper towels.

2 Place the potatoes on a baking tray. Drizzle with olive oil. Salt to taste. Bake 30 minutes, until golden brown and crispy.

Croquette Potatoes

These are mashed potato parcels shaped into barrels and coated with egg white and matzah meal or bread crumbs. They are a great favorite in my house, and—like latkes—they always disappear quickly. These are usually served as a side dish to fish or chicken. These can be made in advance and refrigerated until ready to use. Just pop them into the oven at 350°–400°F for 10 minutes to reheat them.

PAREVE: contains no meat or dairy products / Passover-friendly / can be made in advance
PREPARATION TIME: 20 minutes / **COOKING TIME:** 15 minutes / **MAKES:** about 20 croquettes

**8 boiling potatoes, boiled and peeled ◆ 2 large eggs, separated
3 tablespoons melted margarine ◆ 1 teaspoon freshly grated nutmeg
3 tablespoons finely snipped chives ◆ Salt
Freshly ground black pepper ◆ 1 cup medium-ground matzah meal or bread crumbs
About 4 to 6 cups vegetable oil ◆ Fresh chive blades, for garnish**

1 Place the potatoes in a large bowl or pot. Using a potato ricer, mash the potatoes until very smooth.

2 Add the egg yolks, margarine, nutmeg, and snipped chives. Salt and pepper to taste. Stir to mix.

3 Using a fork, lightly whisk the egg whites. Place in a small shallow dish.

4 Place the matzah meal or bread crumbs in a shallow dish.

5 Using wet hands, take 2 tablespoons mashed potato and mold into barrel shapes. Roll in the egg white, then in matzah meal or bread crumbs.

6 Heat the vegetable oil in a deep-fat fryer or a large, deep skillet over medium heat until the oil is 350°F (or until a small piece of bread dropped into the oil fries to a crisp in 30 seconds).

7 Place the croquettes (in batches, if necessary) in the fryer and cook 5 to 7 minutes, until golden brown and crispy. Blot with paper towels. Serve garnished with chives.

Kasha with Mushrooms

Kasha, also known as buckwheat groats, was a popular dish with the poorer Jews in Russia in the early nineteenth century. It is nutritious, high in fiber, and low in fat. I like to serve it with tongue, braised brisket, Pot Roast (see page 58), and Roast Chicken (see page 57). Kasha can be purchased in fine, medium, or coarse grain. If you're looking for a traditional dish, coarse grain is the one to use. The secret to creating a wonderful kasha dish is to toast the grains before they are baked. Toasted kasha is available at some supermarkets—it provides a shortcut to creating this dish, but you can easily toast kasha yourself.

FLEISHIK: contains meat *or* **PAREVE:** contains no meat or dairy products
PREPARATION TIME: 20 minutes / **COOKING TIME:** 1 hour / **SERVES:** 8

2¼ cups coarse-grain kasha (buckwheat groats) ◆ 1 large egg, lightly beaten
4½ cups chicken stock (fleishik) or vegetable stock (pareve) ◆ ¼ cup vegetable oil
2 large yellow onions, peeled and chopped finely
2 cups white mushrooms, cleaned and chopped coarsely ◆ 4 tablespoons fresh parsley,
chopped coarsely (reserve 3 to 4 sprigs for garnish)
1 teaspoon fine sea salt ◆ Freshly ground black pepper ◆ 2 tablespoons extra-virgin olive oil

◆

1 Preheat the oven to 350°F.

2 Place the kasha in a large frying pan over medium heat. Toast, stirring constantly, until the kasha gives off an aroma (about 5 minutes). Immediately add the egg and stir vigorously into the kasha. Add the chicken or vegetable stock. Stir to mix.

3 Transfer the mixture to a baking dish and bake covered 45 minutes.

4 Meanwhile, heat the vegetable oil in a medium frying pan over medium heat. Add the onions and mushrooms. Sauté until the onions are soft and the mushroom liquid has been reabsorbed (about 10 minutes). Stir in the chopped parsley and cook 1 minute. Generously salt and pepper. Set aside.

5 Remove kasha from the oven. Stir in the onion-mushroom mixture. Transfer to a serving bowl. Drizzle with olive oil and garnish with parsley.

Homemade Coleslaw

*A simcha (party) just isn't a simcha without coleslaw. This versatile, tasty dish is
often served on Shabbat, as well as during Passover.*

PAREV: contains no meat or dairy products / Passover-friendly / can be made in advance
PREPARATION TIME: 5 minutes / **COOKING TIME:** 0 minutes / **SERVES:** 8 people

4 cups coarsely shredded white cabbage leaves
4 cups coarsely shredded red cabbage leaves
3 medium carrots, peeled and grated coarse
⅓ cup chopped walnuts (if desired)
2 cups mayonnaise
Juice of ½ medium lemon
1 tablespoon honey
1 teaspoon prepared whole-grain or Dijon mustard ◆ Salt
Freshly ground black pepper
12 endive leaves or 6 radicchio leaves
6 green savoy cabbage leaves

◆

Mama says...
As a variation on this classic coleslaw,
try adding 1/3 cup white raisins to the
coleslaw for extra sweetness.

1 In a large bowl, toss together cabbage, carrots, and (if desired) walnuts. Set aside.

2 Place mayonnaise, lemon juice, honey, and mustard in a medium bowl. Salt and pepper to taste. Mix thoroughly.

3 Add the fresh dressing to the cabbage mixture and stir thoroughly to mix.

4 Transfer to a serving dish, garnish with endive or radicchio and savoy cabbage leaves, and serve.

Vegetable Couscous

My friend Sharon gave me this Sephardi recipe. This dish hails from Tunisia, where Sharon's mother-in-law lived until persecution led them to flee to Tiberias in Northern Israel. Times were tough—they lived in a wooden hut, and meat was scarce. Fortunately, vegetables were plentiful, and the family enjoyed them in this dish frequently. Years later—in another country and another culture—we still enjoy its delightful colors, textures, and flavors. The traditional way to eat this is to drain off most of the couscous "soup," garnish it with a few chickpeas, and have it as a first course. The vegetables are placed on top of the couscous, and this is eaten as the main course, accompanied by pickled vegetables. Today, we like to serve this as a colorful side dish to roast meats and fish. This dish calls for a very deep pan, as it requires a lot of liquid to produce both the side dish and the "soup" that can be used as a first course. If you prefer to omit the "soup" part, reduce the amount of vegetable stock used to cook the vegetables to 6 cups (so that 8½ total cups of vegetable stock are required for the recipe), and drain off and discard the liquid from the cooked vegetables.

PAREVE: contains no meat or dairy products / can be made in advance
PREPARATION TIME: 30 minutes / **COOKING TIME:** 25 minutes / **SERVES:** 10 to 12

¼ cup, plus 3 tablespoons olive oil, divided
3 large carrots, peeled and cut into thin sticks, 2½ inches long
2 celery stalks, cut into 3-inch-long sticks ◆ 1 medium zucchini, cut into 1-inch-thick circles
1 medium yellow onion, peeled and cut into 2-inch-thick wedges
1 medium white cabbage (about 8 ounces), cored and cut into 2-inch-thick wedges
1 medium potato, peeled and chopped coarsely ◆ 1 small butternut squash (about
1 pound), peeled and cut into 2-inch-thick wedges
½ teaspoon turmeric ◆ 11½ cups vegetable stock, divided ◆ Juice of 1 lemon
1 cinnamon stick ◆ Salt ◆ Freshly ground black pepper ◆ One 14-ounce can chickpeas, drained
2½ cups couscous ◆ 4 tablespoons parsley, for garnish

1 Heat ¼ cup olive oil in a large, deep (4-quart or larger) saucepan over medium heat. Add the carrots, celery, zucchini, onion, cabbage, potato, and squash. Sauté 10 minutes, stirring frequently.

2 Stir in turmeric. Add 9 cups vegetable stock, lemon juice, and cinnamon stick. Generously salt and pepper to taste.

3 Increase the heat to medium-high and bring to a boil. Reduce the heat to medium-low and simmer until all the vegetables are soft (about 20 minutes).

4 Bring to a boil and simmer for 20 minutes or until the vegetables are quite soft. Remove from the heat.

5 Set aside 2 tablespoons chickpeas. Add the remaining chickpeas to the vegetables. Stir and set aside.

6 Place the couscous in a deep, heat-resistant dish. In a small saucepan, bring the remaining 2½ cups of vegetable stock to a boil over medium-high heat. Pour the stock over the couscous. Immediately seal the dish with plastic wrap. Let sit 5 minutes.

7 Using a fork, fluff the couscous. Stir in the remaining 3 tablespoons of olive oil. Salt and pepper to taste.

8 Place a large colander over a large saucepan or pot. Drain the vegetables. Remove and discard the cinnamon stick.

9 Transfer the "soup" to individual bowls, garnish with the reserved chickpeas, and serve (or refrigerate the "soup" up to 2 days for later use).

10 Transfer the couscous to a large serving platter. Top with the vegetable-chickpea mixture. Garnish with parsley sprigs and serve hot.

chapter five

FRIDAY NIGHT
DESSERTS

Lemon Meringue Pie

This is a satisfying, sweet, light finish to any Friday night dinner. Although it can be made using cookies as its base, I prefer a real, old-fashioned pie crust.

PAREVE: contains no meat or dairy products / can be made in advance
PREPARATION TIME: 25 minutes (plus 30 minutes to chill) / **COOKING TIME:** 1 hour
SERVES: 6

PIE CRUST DOUGH
2¼ cups all-purpose flour ◆ 1 cup nondairy margarine ◆ 1 large egg
Zest of 1 medium organic lemon, grated finely ◆ 2 tablespoons confectioners' sugar

FILLING
½ cup cornstarch ◆ 4 cups cold soy milk
Yolks of 5 large eggs (whites reserved for meringue)
2 to 3 tablespoons superfine sugar, to taste
Juice and grated zest of 2 medium organic lemons

MERINGUE
Whites of 5 large eggs ◆ 1¼ cups superfine sugar

◆

1 Make the pie crust dough. Place all the ingredients in a food processor that is fitted with a dough blade. Process until the dough forms a ball. Transfer the dough to a work surface, wrap in plastic wrap, and flatten so it is 1-inch thick. Refrigerate 30 minutes.

2 Preheat the oven to 400°F.

3 Lightly flour a work surface. Remove the dough from the plastic wrap and roll out to fit a 2-inch-deep, 10-inch round springform pie plate. Gently ease the dough into the pie plate.

4 Cover the pie crust dough with aluminum foil. Place some baking beans on the aluminum foil. Bake blind 30 minutes.

5 Make the filling. In a medium bowl, mix together the cornstarch and 2 tablespoons soy milk. Heat the remaining soy milk in a medium-sized saucepan over medium heat. Pour the hot milk into the cornstarch mixture and stir well.

Return the mixture to the saucepan and, stirring constantly, bring to a boil over medium heat. Boil 3 to 4 minutes, stirring constantly.

6 In a small bowl, whisk together the egg yolks and sugar until thick and creamy. Add the milk mixture and stir to blend. Stir in the lemon juice and zest. Immediately pour into the cooked pie crust. Set aside to cool.

7 Reduce the oven temperature to 325°F.

8 Make the meringue. Place the egg whites in a clean, medium-sized bowl. Whisk until stiff, but not dry. Whisking constantly, add the sugar 1 tablespoon at a time, until all the sugar has been incorporated into the meringue.

9 Spoon or pipe the meringue high onto the pie filling, completely covering the pie filling.

10 Bake 20 minutes or until the meringue is pale and lightly browned.

Mama says...
To create a perfect meringue, be sure to add the sugar to the egg whites very gradually, whisking constantly.

Apple-Plum Crumble

This is a great fall dessert, when apples and plums are plentiful. I love to serve this with hot Nondairy Custard (see page 93).

PAREVE: contains no meat or dairy products / can be made in advance
PREPARATION TIME: 30 minutes / **COOKING TIME:** 30 minutes / **SERVES:** 8 to 10

FRUIT MIXTURE

2 medium red or green sweet apples, peeled, cored, and sliced thinly
About 15 plums, pitted and sliced thin
1 tablespoon cinnamon ◆ 2 tablespoons raw sugar or dark brown sugar
2 tablespoons all-purpose flour

CRUMBLE

2 cups all-purpose flour ◆ 1 packed cup light brown sugar ◆ ¾ cup margarine
1 cup oats ◆ 1 tablespoon cinnamon ◆ 2 teaspoons baking powder
2 tablespoons shredded dried coconut

◆

1 Preheat the oven to 400°F.

2 Make the fruit mixture. Place the apples and plums in a large bowl. Add the cinnamon, sugar, and flour. Gently mix. Transfer the mixture to a large baking dish.

3 Make the crumble. Place all the ingredients in a food processor. Process until the mixture forms crumbs. Sprinkle the crumbs evenly over the fruit mixture.

4 Bake uncovered for 30 minutes.

Mama says...
For an even better-tasting, crunchier crumble, cook the crumble in advance, then reheat it when you are ready to prepare the dessert.

Chocolate Roulade

This is an easy-to-make sponge cake that is filled with cream cheese and grated chocolate, then rolled. For a delicious pareve dessert, use nondairy cream cheese.

MILCHIK: contains dairy products *or* **PAREVE:** contains no meat or dairy products
can be made in advance / Passover-friendly
PREPARATION TIME: 25 minutes (plus about 30 minutes to cool)
COOKING TIME: 15 minutes / **SERVES:** 6 to 8

¼ cup good-quality bittersweet chocolate ◆ 6 large eggs, separated
½ cup superfine sugar ◆ 2 tablespoons cocoa ◆ 2 teaspoons vanilla extract
2 cups cream cheese (milchik), heavy cream—whipped for Passover, or nondairy
cream cheese substitute (pareve) ◆ ¼ cup, plus 2 tablespoons grated bittersweet chocolate
1 cup raspberries (if desired) ◆ ¼ cup confectioners' sugar

◆

1 Preheat the oven to 350°F. Line a 9-inch by 13-inch jelly-roll pan with parchment paper.

2 Melt the chocolate in a double boiler.

3 In a large bowl, whisk together the egg yolks and superfine sugar until thick and creamy. Stir in the cocoa and melted chocolate.

4 In a medium bowl, whisk the egg whites until very stiff. Stir in the vanilla extract. Gently fold into the chocolate mixture. Pour into the pan and spread evenly to the edges of the pan.

5 Bake 15 minutes or until the mixture has risen and is firm to touch.

6 Invert onto a clean piece of parchment paper. Peel off the parchment-paper lining. Set aside until cool (about 30 minutes).

7 In a medium bowl, mix together the cream cheese or nondairy cream cheese substitute and the grated chocolate. Add the raspberries, if desired. Stir in the confectioners' sugar last.

8 Carefully spread the chocolate mixture over the cooled cake. Starting at one of the wider ends, carefully roll up the cake (use the parchment paper to help guide the cake). Using a spatula or a cake slicer, carefully transfer to a serving platter.

Mama's Best-Ever Apple Pie

*Apple pie is a common, beloved dessert on Friday evenings. The cinnamon
permeates the apple, giving the pie a wonderful flavor. This particular recipe creates
an old-fashioned, double-crusted treat. I love to serve it with hot Nondairy Custard.*

PAREVE: contains no meat or dairy products / can be made in advance / can be frozen up to 2 weeks
PREPARATION TIME: 40 minutes (plus 30 minutes to allow pastry to rest) / **COOKING TIME:** 40 minutes
MAKES: One 9-inch pie

PIE CRUST DOUGH
2½ cups all-purpose flour ◆ ½ cup margarine ◆ 1 teaspoon salt ◆ 2 teaspoons cinnamon
2 tablespoons superfine sugar ◆ 1 large egg ◆ 3 tablespoons cold water

GLAZE
Yolks of 1 to 2 large eggs, lightly beaten

FILLING
6 medium Granny Smith apples, peeled, cored, and sliced thinly ◆ 1 tablespoon cinnamon
2 tablespoons all-purpose flour ◆ 2 tablespoons dark brown sugar
Juice of ½ medium lemon ◆ 1 tablespoon margarine, cut into small pieces

◆

1 Make the pie crust dough. Place all the ingredients in a food processor that is fitted with a dough blade. Process to form a dough.

2 Remove the dough, wrap in plastic wrap, and flatten to 1-inch thick. Refrigerate for 30 minutes.

3 Preheat the oven to 400°F. Lightly flour a work surface. Remove the dough from the refrigerator and unwrap. Transfer two-thirds of the dough to the work surface. Rewrap the remaining dough and set aside.

4 Roll out the pastry to fit a 1-inch-deep, 9-inch round pie plate (allow for a bit of overlap).

5 Gently place the dough over the pie plate and ease into the plate. Brush the edges of the dough with the egg yolk glaze just before the top dough is put on the pie.

6 Make the filling. Place all the ingredients in a large bowl and gently mix. Place the filling in the pie. Set aside.

7 Make the pie dough top. Lightly flour the work surface. Transfer the remaining dough to the work surface and roll it out to fit the pie plate (allow for a bit of overlap). Gently place on top of the pie filling. Squeeze together the dough edges to seal. Glaze the dough with the remaining egg yolk.

8 Using a sharp knife, cut three curved slits in the top layer of the dough (to allow steam to escape).

9 Bake for 40 minutes or until the pie crust is golden brown.

Nondairy Custard

PAREVE: contains no meat or dairy products / **PREPARATION TIME:** 10 minutes
COOKING TIME: 15 minutes / **SERVES:** 10 (makes about 2½ cups)

Yolks of 6 large eggs ◆ ½ cup superfine sugar ◆ 2½ cups soy milk
2 teaspoons vanilla extract
2 tablespoons custard powder (available at specialty food stores and at some grocery stores)

◆

1 Place the egg yolks and sugar in a medium-sized bowl. Beat until pale and thick.

2 Place the soy milk in a medium-sized saucepan. Bring to a boil over medium heat. Remove from the heat.

3 In a small bowl or glass, mix together the custard powder and 2 tablespoons hot soy milk. Whisking constantly, pour the mixture into the soy milk. Pour the soy milk mixture into the egg mixture. Stir to mix.

4 Return the mixture to the saucepan and heat over low heat, stirring constantly, until the mixture thickens and coats the back of a spoon (about 10 minutes).

Berry-Peach Salad

There is always a place for fruit at the Jewish table. Use the ripest berries you can find for the best flavor.

PAREVE: contains no meat or dairy products / Passover-friendly / can be made in advance
PREPARATION TIME: 15 minutes (plus 2 hours to chill) / **COOKING TIME:** 0 minutes
SERVES: 6 to 8

3 medium, very ripe peaches ◆ 2 cups fresh blueberries, rinsed
1 cup fresh blackberries, rinsed ◆ 2 cups fresh raspberries, rinsed ◆ ½ cup sugar
1 teaspoon cinnamon ◆ 2 tablespoons Kiddush wine or kir
Fresh mint leaves, for decoration

◆

1 Remove and discard the pits from the peaches. Cut the peaches into small segments. Place in a large bowl. Add the blueberries, blackberries, and 1 cup raspberries and gently toss to mix. Set aside.

2 Pulse the sugar and remaining raspberries in a food processor or a blender until puréed. Pour the mixture through a very fine strainer into a bowl.

3 Add the cinnamon and wine or kir to the freshly puréed berries. Stir to mix. Pour over the fruit mixture and gently toss to mix. Chill in the refrigerator for 2 hours.

4 Spoon the mixture into individual glass dishes or Champagne glasses. Decorate with mint leaves and serve with Mandelbrot (see page 113).

Chocolate Pavlova with Raspberries

This recipe has been in my family for years, but it has been adapted over time to take advantage of modern cooking techniques and availability of key ingredients. Strawberries, blueberries, peaches, or nectarines can be combined with the whipping cream, but my favorite remains fresh raspberries. Frozen or canned raspberries may be used as well, provided they are thawed, if frozen, and well drained.

PAREVE: contains no meat or dairy products / must be made 1 to 2 days in advance
PREPARATION TIME: 25 minutes / **COOKING TIME:** 2 hours / **SERVES:** 8 to 10

Whites of 6 large eggs ◆ 1 cup superfine sugar, divided
2 tablespoons cornstarch or potato flour ◆ 1 teaspoon vanilla extract
2 teaspoons white wine vinegar ◆ 1 cup coarsely grated bittersweet chocolate
1 cup nondairy whipped topping ◆ 1 cup raspberries

◆

1 Preheat the oven to 225°F. Line a large baking tray with parchment paper. Set aside.

2 In a large bowl, whisk the egg whites until stiff. Whisking constantly, gradually add ⅔ cup sugar, 1 tablespoon at a time.

3 Sift in the cornstarch or potato flour and the remaining sugar. Continue to whisk the egg whites. Stir in the vanilla extract and vinegar. Whisk again. Fold in the chocolate.

4 Spoon or pipe the mixture into a 9-inch circle on the lined baking tray.

5 Bake 2 hours. Turn off the oven and let sit in the oven until completely cooled (about 40 minutes).

6 Transfer cooled meringue to a serving platter.

7 Place whipped topping in a medium bowl. Fold in the raspberries. Spoon onto meringue and serve.

Hot Chocolate Soufflé Pudding

Everyone loves chocolate soufflé pudding, and this recipe is perfect for family Friday nights. Coated with a trufflelike chocolate sauce, this cocoa-based pudding will satisfy any chocoholic. Quick and easy to make, it can also be made in advance and reheated.

PAREVE: contains no meat or dairy products / can be made in advance
PREPARATION TIME: 25 minutes / **COOKING TIME:** 35 minutes / **SERVES:** 6

SOUFFLÉ PUDDING

1 tablespoon margarine ◆ 3 tablespoons hot water ◆ ⅓ cup bittersweet chocolate
1½ cups self-rising flour ◆ 1 teaspoon baking powder ◆ ½ teaspoon baking soda
½ cup sugar ◆ 3 tablespoons cocoa ◆ 4 large eggs ◆ 1 cup soy milk
2 tablespoons corn syrup ◆ 1 cup sunflower oil

SAUCE

⅓ cup margarine ◆ ¾ cup plain bittersweet chocolate ◆ ¾ cup soy cream
1¼ cups confectioners' sugar

◆

1 Preheat the oven to 350°F. Grease with the margarine and line a 7½-inch by 3-inch-deep, round cake pan.

2 Melt the chocolate for the soufflé pudding. Place in a food processor with 3 tablespoons hot water and whip together.

3 Make the pudding. Sift together the flour, baking powder, baking soda, cocoa, and sugar into a large bowl. Add the melted chocolate, eggs, soy milk, corn syrup, and sunflower oil. Beat until smooth. Pour into the cake pan.

4 Bake 25 minutes or until the pudding has risen and is springy to touch.

5 Make the sauce. Place the margarine, chocolate, and soy cream in a medium-sized saucepan and melt over low heat. Whisk until smooth. Remove from the heat.

6 Sift a third of the confectioners' sugar into the mixture. Whisk until smooth. Repeat until the sauce is glossy.

7 Invert the pudding onto a warm serving plate. Cut thick slices and pour the sauce over.

Lokshen Kugel

Lokshen kugel, or noodle pudding, is an unusual and exclusively Jewish way of eating pasta as a dessert! It may sound strange, but my children are addicted to it, and the sweet ingredients make for a very filling and satisfying dessert. Although Lokshen kugel can easily be reheated, or even served cold, we find that it rarely lasts beyond Friday night. This particular recipe is really quick and easy, and it's extremely delicious. I like to use flat egg noodles that are at least ½-inch wide.

PAREVE: contains no meat or dairy products / can be made in advance
PREPARATION TIME: 20 minutes / **COOKING TIME:** 40 minutes / **SERVES:** 8

¾ cup margarine ◆ 1 tablespoon salt ◆ 3 cups egg noodles ◆ ½ teaspoon baking soda
4 red or green sweet apples, peeled, cored, and grated coarsely ◆ 1½ cups superfine sugar
2 teaspoons cinnamon ◆ 4 large eggs, lightly beaten ◆ 1 teaspoon vanilla extract
3 tablespoons dark raisins ◆ 3 tablespoons apricot jam ◆ 1 tablespoon water

◆

1 Preheat the oven to 350°F.

2 Using 1 tablespoon margarine, grease a 2-inch-deep, 9-inch by 14-inch baking dish. Set aside.

3 Fill a large saucepan with water. Add the salt. Bring to a boil. Add the noodles and cook until al dente (about 5 minutes). Drain and place in a large bowl.

4 Melt the remaining margarine in a small saucepan over low heat. Toss into the noodles. Add the apples, sugar, cinnamon, baking soda, eggs, vanilla extract, and raisins. Place the mixture in a baking dish.

5 Bake 35 to 40 minutes or until golden brown.

6 Place the jam and water in a small saucepan and melt over low heat. Stir to mix. Drizzle the mixture onto the kugel.

Mama says...
Dust individual serving plates with cinnamon. Spoon a generous helping of kugel onto plates and serve.

Baklava

This is a traditional Middle Eastern dessert that features layers of phyllo filled with chopped nuts and honey syrup. Despite being rather sweet, it is quite irresistible. I serve it with pareve vanilla "ice cream" or with coffee or lemon tea on Friday evenings. For a true Sephardi dessert, serve this with Turkish coffee or mint tea. Baklava is expensive to buy, and you may think that it's difficult to make at home. However, I promise that my recipe is not challenging, that it is economical, and that it serves a large number of guests.

MILCHIK: contains dairy products / can be made in advance / can be frozen up to 1 month
PREPARATION TIME: 30 minutes (plus 30 minutes to chill) / **COOKING TIME:** 30 minutes
SERVES: 10 to 12

1 tablespoon unsalted butter, for greasing, plus 2 cups, melted
¾ cup blanched almonds ♦ ¾ cup raw pistachios
1 cup sugar, divided ♦ 12 sheets (about 16 ounces) phyllo, thawed if frozen
¾ cup honey ♦ 1 cup water
¼ cup rosewater ♦ 2 tablespoons lemon juice

♦

Mama says...
Decorate baklava with coarsely chopped pistachio nuts. Serve with yogurt.

1 Grease with butter and line a 12-inch by 8-inch jelly-roll pan. Set aside.

2 Place the almonds, pistachios, and ½ cup sugar in a food processor. Pulse to chop rough.

3 Cut the phyllo to fit the baking pan. Place one layer phyllo on the bottom of the pan. Brush with melted butter. Repeat twice. Sprinkle 3 tablespoons of the nut mixture evenly over the third layer of the phyllo.

4 Repeat until all the phyllo sheets are used, finishing with three layers of phyllo on the top. Refrigerate 30 minutes.

5 Preheat the oven to 350°F.

6 Using a sharp knife, cut the chilled baklava in diagonal strips. Cut across the strips to form diamond shapes.

7 Bake 25 to 30 minutes or until golden brown.

8 Meanwhile, place the honey, water, rosewater, and lemon juice in a medium saucepan. Heat on low 10 minutes. Remove from the heat and cool.

9 Using a sharp knife, cut the baklava pieces again. Pour the syrup over the baklava. Serve hot, warm, or chilled.

chapter six
TEA AT BOOBA'S

Booba's Dried Fruit Strudel

This is one of my mother's recipes and she received it from her mother. It's easy, and it makes a little piece of dough and some dried fruit go a long way.

MILCHIK: contains dairy products *or* **PAREVE:** contains no meat or dairy products
can be made in advance / can be frozen up to 1 month
PREPARATION TIME: 25 minutes (plus 30 minutes to chill)
COOKING TIME: 20 minutes (plus 10 minutes to cool before serving) / **MAKES:** 35 pieces

3½ cups self-rising flour ◆ 1 cup unsalted butter (milchik) or margarine ◆ 2 large eggs
1 to 2 tablespoons cold water ◆ 4 to 6 tablespoons raspberry or black currant jam
2 cups mixed dried fruit, such as raisins, currants, and dried cranberries
½ cup candied cherries, halved (available at specialty food stores and at some grocery stores)
½ cup chopped walnuts ◆ 2 teaspoons cinnamon

◆

1 Place the flour, butter, eggs, and 1 to 2 tablespoons water in a food processor that is fitted with a dough blade. Process, adding the remaining water, a bit at a time, if necessary, until the dough is soft and smooth. Remove the dough from the food processor, wrap in plastic wrap, and flatten to 1-inch thick. Refrigerate 30 minutes.

2 Preheat the oven to 350°F. Line a baking tray with parchment paper. Set aside.

3 Lightly flour a work surface. Cut the dough into four equal-sized portions. Place one portion on the work surface. Using a hand roller, roll out the dough into a 13½-inch by 6-inch rectangle. Cover the remaining dough with plastic wrap.

4 Spread a thin layer of jam over the entire surface of the dough. Sprinkle ¼ dried fruit, cherries, and walnuts evenly over the dough, and repeat with the remaining portions of dough.

5 Fold each of the dough's long sides 1 inch. Starting at one short side, roll up the dough, so that it resembles a jelly roll.

6 Place the dough on the baking tray. Cut small slits in 1-inch intervals in the dough to allow steam to escape. Sprinkle cinnamon onto dough.

7 Bake 20 minutes or until golden brown and firm to touch. Let cool to room temperature, about 10 minutes.

Ultimate Apple Cake

Certain recipes become family heirlooms that are treasured by generations. This is definitely one of those. All of my sisters have this recipe. Although we have tried out many variations, using plums, apricots, and pears, the cake just seems perfect with apples. It is suitable for serving at tea and as a hot or cold after-meal dessert.

PAREVE: contains no meat or dairy products / can be made in advance / can be frozen up to 2 weeks
PREPARATION TIME: 20 minutes / **COOKING TIME:** 70 minutes / **SERVES:** 8

1 tablespoon vegetable oil ◆ 2 large eggs ◆ 1 cup superfine sugar ◆ ½ cup margarine
1½ teaspoons baking powder ◆ 1 teaspoon almond extract ◆ 1 cup self-rising flour
4 to 5 sweet, green, medium apples, peeled, cored, and sliced very thinly
1 tablespoon vanilla sugar ◆ 1 tablespoon light brown sugar, for decoration (if desired)

◆

1 Preheat the oven to 350°F.

2 Grease with vegetable oil and line an 8½-inch round springform cake pan. Set aside.

3 Place the eggs and superfine sugar in the bowl of an electric mixer. Mix until blended.

4 Melt the margarine in a small saucepan over low heat. Add the melted margarine, baking powder, and almond extract to egg-sugar mixture.

5 While mixing, slowly add the flour. Mix until well blended (mixture should be very thick).

6 Put two-thirds batter in the cake pan. Top with the apples, completely covering the batter. Top the apples with the remaining batter (the batter will not completely cover the apples).

7 Sprinkle the vanilla sugar over the top of the batter.

8 Bake until the cake is golden brown and a toothpick inserted into the center of the cake comes out clean (50 to 60 minutes). Remove from the oven and let cool to warm.

9 If desired, sprinkle with brown sugar just before serving.

Booba's Kiddush Kichels

These simple little cookies bring back memories of fun visits to my grandparents' house for Shabbat tea. They are quick to make, and they keep well in an airtight container for 4 to 5 days. In this recipe, I call for vanilla and almond extracts to flavor the cookies, but a pinch of dried ginger, allspice, or cinnamon would make a pleasant alternative.

MILCHIK: contains dairy products / can be made in advance / can be frozen up to 2 months
PREPARATION TIME: 15 minutes / **COOKING TIME:** 20 minutes / **MAKES:** about 55 cookies

1 cup unsalted butter ◆ Yolk of 1 large egg ◆ ¾ cup confectioners' sugar
2 cups all-purpose flour ◆ About ¾ cup ground almonds ◆ ½ teaspoon salt
1 teaspoon vanilla extract ◆ 1 teaspoon almond extract

◆

1 Preheat the oven to 350°F. Line a baking tray with parchment paper. Set aside.

2 In a medium bowl, cream the butter. Beating constantly, gradually add all the remaining ingredients.

3 Shape the dough into small balls (each about the size of a teaspoon). Place carefully on the baking tray.

4 Bake 15 to 20 minutes or until firm to touch. Do not allow to brown.

Mama says...
For added visual excitement, create these in different shapes—cut circles in half to make crescents, or lightly roll out the dough and use cookie cutters to make any shapes you desire. These may also be decorated with candied cherries or nuts.

Oatmeal Cookies

This is an old recipe that I inherited from my grandmother's sister. These cookies are extremely delicious. Fortunately, the ingredients are relatively healthful.

MILCHIK: contains dairy products *or* **PAREVE:** contains no meat or dairy products
can be made in advance / can be frozen up to 1 month
PREPARATION TIME: 15 minutes (plus 30 minutes to chill) / **COOKING TIME:** 15 to 20 minutes
MAKES: about 55 cookies

1 cup honey
9 tablespoons unsalted butter (milchik) or margarine ◆ 6¼ cups rolled oats
1 cup whole-wheat flour ◆ 1 teaspoon baking soda ◆ 2 teaspoons cinnamon

◆

1 Preheat the oven to 350°F. Line 2 baking trays with parchment paper. Set aside.

2 In a large bowl, cream together the honey and butter or margarine. Stir in the oats, flour, baking soda, and cinnamon.

3 Wrap the dough in plastic wrap and refrigerate for 30 minutes.

4 Roll 1 tablespoon of the mixture into a ball. Gently flatten and place on a baking tray. Repeat, leaving 1 inch of space between the cookies on the baking trays.

5 Bake for 15 to 20 minutes, until golden and set.

Mama says...
Just before serving, dust cookies with confectioners' sugar.

Chocolate Marble Cake

This is a very traditional Jewish cake. Although it is quite plain, it is addictive. My family calls this the "cut and come again" cake, because everybody always goes back for seconds! It is also good for small children, as it contains no nuts or strong flavors. Try it warm from the oven—the cake melts in your mouth.

MILCHIK: contains dairy products *or* **PAREVE:** contains no meat or dairy products
can be made in advance / can be frozen up to 1 month
PREPARATION TIME: 15 minutes / **COOKING TIME:** 40 minutes / **SERVES:** 8

1 tablespoon vegetable oil ◆ 4 ounces bittersweet chocolate
2 tablespoons milk (milchik) or soy milk (pareve) ◆ ¾ cup self-rising flour ◆ 2 large eggs
¾ cup superfine sugar ◆ ¾ cup margarine, softened ◆ 1 teaspoon vanilla extract

◆

1 Preheat the oven to 350°F. Grease with vegetable oil and line an 8-inch-round springform cake pan.

2 Melt the chocolate in a double boiler over medium heat. Add the milk or soy milk and mix well. Remove from the heat and let cool to room temperature.

3 In a large bowl, mix together the flour and sugar. Add the eggs, margarine, and vanilla extract. Mix well.

4 Place the batter in the pan. Drop spoonfuls of chocolate batter on top. Using a wooden skewer or a spoon, swirl the chocolate into the cake batter to give it a marbled effect.

5 Bake 35 to 40 minutes or until a wooden toothpick inserted into the cake comes out clean.

Carrot Cake

Healthful eating is not normally high on the agenda during tea at Grandma's, but this yummy carrot cake manages to combine the best of both worlds—great taste and nutritious ingredients (and no butter or cream)! I love the combination of crushed pineapple, carrots, and walnuts—not only does it make this cake taste delicious, but it also creates a wonderfully moist texture. This is an ideal treat to pack in lunch boxes and picnic baskets.

PAREVE: contains no meat or dairy products / can be made in advance / can be frozen up to 1 month
PREPARATION TIME: 15 minutes / **COOKING TIME:** 1 hour / **SERVES:** 8

1 tablespoon vegetable oil ◆ 1 cup all-purpose flour ◆ ¾ cup superfine sugar
1 teaspoon baking soda ◆ 1 teaspoon baking powder ◆ 1 teaspoon cinnamon
2 large eggs ◆ 1 cup vegetable oil ◆ 1 cup grated carrots
1 cup crushed pineapple with juice ◆ ⅓ cup walnut pieces

◆

1 Preheat the oven to 350°F. Grease with vegetable oil and line a 9-inch round springform cake pan. Set aside.

2 In a large bowl, mix together the flour, sugar, baking soda, baking powder, and cinnamon.

Add the eggs and vegetable oil. Mix well. Stir in the carrots, pineapple, and walnuts.

3 Bake 1 hour or until golden brown and a toothpick inserted into the center of the cake comes out clean.

Mama says...
Just before serving, dust the cake with a bit of confectioners' sugar.

Lamington Squares

In the 1960s my grandmother went to South Africa to visit relatives. When she came back she brought this recipe with her. Today my mother still makes this for special teas. We all love its combination of ingredients and the contrast of flavors that a plain sponge cake, coated in chocolate and dipped in coconut, offers.

MILCHIK: contains dairy products *or* **PAREVE:** contains no meat or dairy products
can be made in advance / can be frozen up to 1 month
PREPARATION TIME: 20 minutes / **COOKING TIME:** 20 minutes / **MAKES:** 36 squares

1 tablespoon vegetable oil ◆ ¼ cup superfine sugar
½ cup unsalted butter (milchik) or margarine (pareve)
2 large eggs ◆ ½ cup milk (milchik) or soy milk (pareve) ◆ ½ teaspoon baking soda
1 teaspoon cream of tartar ◆ Zest of 1 medium organic lemon ◆ 1½ cups self-rising flour
1 cup water ◆ ¼ cup cocoa ◆ ¼ cup confectioners' sugar
2 teaspoons vanilla extract ◆ ¼ cup, plus 2 tablespoons shredded coconut

◆

1 Preheat the oven to 350°F. Line and grease with vegetable oil a 9½-inch-square baking pan. Set aside.

2 In a large bowl, cream together the superfine sugar and butter or margarine. Beating constantly, add the eggs, one at a time. Still beating, add the milk or soy milk, baking soda, cream of tartar, and lemon zest.

3 Gradually fold the flour into the mixture. Spoon the mixture into the pan and level off.

4 Bake 20 minutes. Remove from the oven and cut into squares. Set aside to cool.

5 Place the water in a small saucepan and bring to a boil over medium-high heat. Reduce the heat to medium low. Stir in the cocoa, confectioners' sugar, and vanilla extract. Simmer 2 minutes. Remove from the heat and let cool to room temperature.

6 Dip each square of cake into the chocolate mixture and roll in coconut.

Stuffed Monkey

When I was asked to write this book, my mother presented me with a little black book that had belonged to a great-great-aunt who had lived to well into her nineties. Inside was a recipe for something called "stuffed monkey." There were no directions; just a list of ingredients. After doing some research and experimenting, I discovered that this is actually a type of sweet pastry sandwich, and I was able to re-create the complete recipe. The dried cranberries are a modern twist, and I think they add just the right finishing touch. Coarsely chopped dried cherries may be substituted for the cranberries, if you wish.

MILCHIK: contains dairy products *or* **PAREVE:** contains no meat or dairy products
PREPARATION TIME: 20 minutes (plus 30 minutes to chill) / **COOKING TIME:** 30 minutes
SERVES: 6

PIE DOUGH
1 tablespoon vegetable oil ◆ 1¼ cups self-rising flour
½ cup unsalted butter (milchik) or margarine
½ cup packed light brown sugar ◆ 1 large egg ◆ 1 teaspoon cinnamon

FILLING
4 tablespoons unsalted butter (milchik) or nondairy margarine (pareve)
¼ cup superfine sugar ◆ Yolks of 2 large eggs (whites reserved for glaze)
¼ cup dried cranberries ◆ ¼ cup white raisins
¼ cup mixed dried, organic citrus peel ◆ About 1½ cups ground almonds

GLAZE
Whites of 2 large eggs

◆

1 Preheat the oven to 375°F. Grease with vegetable oil and line a 1½-inch-deep, 9-inch square baking pan.

2 Make the pie dough. Place all the ingredients in a food processor that is fitted with a dough blade. Process until the dough forms. Remove from the food processor, wrap in plastic wrap, and flatten so that it is about 1-inch thick. Refrigerate 30 minutes.

3 Lightly flour a work surface. Divide the dough into 2 equal portions. Roll out each portion into a square the size of the baking pan (8 inches by 3½ inches). Place one dough square in the bottom of the pan. Set aside the remaining dough square. Cover the remaining dough to prevent it from drying out.

4 Make the filling. Melt the butter in a medium saucepan over medium-low heat. Stir in the sugar, egg yolks, cranberries, raisins, citrus peel, and ground almonds.

5 Spread the filling over the dough square in the cake pan. Top with the remaining dough square. Glaze with egg white.

6 Bake 30 minutes or until golden brown. Let cool before slicing.

Mama says...
Cut into squares and dust with confectioners' sugar.

Mandelbrot

Mandelbrot (Yiddish for "almond bread") are hard almond biscuits that are double baked to create a dry cookie similar to Italian biscotti. In fact, these treats were probably introduced to the Italians by the Spanish Jews. Their unique texture and taste make them perfect for dipping into coffee, tea, punch, wine, and soup. I sometimes like to flavor the mandelbrot with chocolate chips, a variety of different nuts, or dried fruits. This is my favorite version—it's made with chocolate, hazelnuts, and almonds. This recipe makes about 50 cookies—that may seem like a large number, but if your family is like mine, they won't last long!

PAREVE: contains no meat or dairy products / can be made in advance / can be frozen up to 2 months
PREPARATION TIME: 20 minutes (plus 15 minutes to cool) / **COOKING TIME:** 40 minutes
MAKES: about 50 cookies

4 cups all-purpose flour ◆ 1 cup superfine sugar ◆ 1 teaspoon baking powder
½ teaspoon salt ◆ 3 large eggs ◆ 1 teaspoon almond extract
½ cup chocolate chips or coarsely chopped bittersweet chocolate ◆ About 1 cup skinned
hazelnuts, chopped coarsely ◆ About 1 cup blanched whole almonds, chopped coarsely

◆

1 Preheat the oven to 350°F. Line a baking tray with parchment paper. Set aside.

2 Place the flour, sugar, baking powder, salt, eggs, chocolate, and almond extract into a food processor that is fitted with a dough blade. Process until a dough is formed. Stir in the hazelnuts and almonds.

3 Lightly flour a work surface and transfer the dough to the work surface. Divide the dough into three equal portions. Roll each piece into 12-inch-long, 2-inch-wide sausage shapes. Place on a baking tray.

4 Bake 25 minutes or until just firm. Remove from the oven and set aside 10 minutes to cool. (Do not turn off the oven.)

5 Using a serrated knife, cut the "sausages" into ½-inch-thick diagonal slices. Return to the oven.

6 Bake 15 minutes, until the centers are dry and the cookies are crisp and golden brown.

Old-Fashioned Fruit Cake

*This is a very old recipe that my grandmother passed down to me.
My mother remembers having this delicious cake at her aunt's house during tea
more than 60 years ago. I love the addition of cocoa—the hint of chocolate in this
rich fruit cake is just delicious. This cake may be frosted, decorated with chopped
almonds, or served plain. Rich and dense, it's suitable for serving not only at tea,
but also at weddings, bar mitzvahs, and other formal festive occasions.
The cake does take some time—six weeks—to set up (otherwise, it's too fresh
to slice), but the result is well worth the wait. During the weeks that it's setting,
occasionally drizzle brandy over the cake, allowing the liquor to soak into the
fruit and flavor it over time.*

MILCHIK: contains dairy products *or* **PAREVE:** contains no meat or dairy products
must be made at least 6 weeks in advance
PREPARATION TIME: 25 minutes (plus 6 weeks to set) / **COOKING TIME:** 2 hours, 30 minutes
SERVES: 15

1 tablespoon vegetable oil ◆ 1¼ cups unsalted butter (milchik) or margarine
2½ cups self-rising flour ◆ ½ teaspoon salt ◆ 7 large eggs ◆ 1⅓ cups superfine sugar
About 1¼ cups ground almonds ◆ Zest and juice of 1 medium organic lemon
Zest and juice of 1 medium organic orange ◆ 1 tablespoon cocoa
1 teaspoon ground allspice ◆ 1 teaspoon cinnamon ◆ 5 cups dried currants
5 cups white raisins ◆ 1 cup candied cherries, chopped coarsely
1 cup mixed, dried organic citrus peel
6 tablespoons brandy (or rum, if desired), divided

◆

1 Preheat the oven to 325°F. Grease with vegetable oil and line a 10-inch round cake pan.

2 Place the butter, flour, and salt in a food processor and process until well combined. Add the eggs, sugar, almonds, zests and juices of lemon and orange, cocoa, allspice, and cinnamon. Pulse to mix.

3 Transfer the batter to a large bowl. Stir in the currants, raisins, cherries, and citrus peel. Spoon the batter into the cake pan.

4 Bake until the cake is firm to the touch and a wooden skewer inserted into the center of the cake comes out clean (about 2½ hours). Remove from the oven and set aside to cool.

5 Place the cooled cake in an airtight container (or wrap the cake in plastic wrap, then in aluminum foil). Let sit 6 weeks (unrefrigerated), occasionally drizzling 1 tablespoon brandy (or rum) over the cake.

ROSH HASHANAH
"Head of the Year"

"Leshana tova tikotevu."
"May you be inscribed for a good and sweet year."

This is the familiar greeting exchanged by family and friends as they gather to celebrate Rosh Hashanah, which are the two holy days at the start of the Jewish New Year. It is a time of reflection and contemplation as we repent for the sins of the past year, but it is also a time of joy and hope for the year to come, as we pray that God will forgive us and look after us in the future.

The festival is celebrated not only in the synagogue, but also in the home, where the dinner table is often lavishly laid out with fruits of the new season, such as pomegranates, figs, persimmons, apples, and pears. Bowls of honey symbolize the wish for a sweet year and a special golden, coiled, circular challah bread, a sign of the year's cycle—round, complete, and uninterrupted—is torn into chunks for dipping into the honey. Apples are another popular fruit, as their round shape expresses the time of the season, and its sweetness reflects the hope for a sweet new year. Combining these two symbolic foods, I like to include apple and honey in the making of my challah during the time from Rosh Hashanah to the end of Succot.

Another favorite recipe of mine is chicken tagine, which is made with apples, prunes, and honey, and Tzimmes (see pages 120 to 121), a sweet carrot stew that uses sliced carrots that resemble coins in the hope that we will be blessed with a prosperous New Year. Honey cake, Lekach (see page 122), is another predominant feature at the festival table and every Jewish mama will have her own variation on the recipe.

Honey-Roasted Chicken

Apple and honey represent our wishes for a good, sweet new year. This popular, family-friendly recipe captures both of these ingredients in one dish. The glaze, which is made with apple juice and honey, gives the chicken a beautiful, crispy coating.

FLEISHIK: contains meat / Passover-friendly / can be made in advance
PREPARATION TIME: 15 minutes / **COOKING TIME:** 85 minutes / **SERVES:** 6

½ cup apple juice ♦ ½ cup dry white wine
¼ cup, plus 1 tablespoon honey, divided ♦ One 5-pound whole chicken
Salt ♦ Freshly ground black pepper
1 medium yellow onion, peeled and chopped coarsely
4 medium red or green apples, peeled, cored, and cut into thick wedges

♦

1 Preheat the oven to 400°F.

2 In a small bowl, whisk together the apple juice, wine, and ¼ cup honey.

3 Place the chicken breast-side down in a large roasting pan. Pour the honey mixture over the chicken. Salt and pepper to taste.

4 Arrange the onions and apples around the chicken. Cover the pan with aluminum foil or use the pan lid.

5 Bake 1 hour.

6 Remove the foil or uncover pan. Bake 15 minutes more.

7 Remove the pan from the oven. Transfer the chicken to a carving board. Let sit 5 minutes.

8 Meanwhile, pour the pan juices into a saucepan. Discard the apples and onions. Add the remaining tablespoon honey and heat over medium-low heat. Cook 10 minutes, stirring frequently. Adjust the seasonings, if desired.

9 Cut the chicken into portions and transfer to a serving platter. Serve with fresh green apple wedges and honey sauce.

Tzimmes

Perhaps it is because sliced carrots symbolize coins that we eat Tzimmes on Rosh Hashanah, when we are hoping to be blessed with a prosperous new year. Although it may be served as a main course, most people think of Tzimmes as a side dish. Although I call for dried apricots, white raisins, or dates, my grandmother's recipe (on which this is based) offers no such alternatives. She was strictly in favor of apricots. The honeyed chicken or vegetable stock softens the fruit (whichever type you choose to use) and gives the dish a delicious flavor.

FLEISHIK: contains meat / Passover-friendly / can be made in advance / can be frozen up to 2 weeks
PREPARATION TIME: 20 minutes / **COOKING TIME:** 50 minutes / **SERVES:** 6

DUMPLINGS
1 cup all-purpose flour or medium-ground matzah meal
2 tablespoons chicken fat or margarine ◆ 2 teaspoons salt ◆ 1 large egg, lightly beaten
1 teaspoon freshly ground black pepper ◆ 2 cups vegetable or chicken stock

STEW
2 tablespoons vegetable oil ◆ 1 medium yellow onion, peeled and chopped coarsely
4 cups thinly sliced carrots ◆ 2½ cups vegetable or chicken stock
2 tablespoons honey ◆ 2 tablespoons lemon juice ◆ 1 teaspoon cinnamon
2 cups dried apricots, white raisins, or dates, or a mixture of these
Salt ◆ Freshly ground black pepper

◆

1 Make the dumplings. In a large bowl, mix together the flour or matzah meal, chicken fat or margarine, and salt and pepper until the mixture resembles fine bread crumbs.

2 Add the egg and 2 cups vegetable or chicken stock and mix together to make a pliable dough. (If necessary, add more stock, a bit at a time.)

3 Roll the dough into walnut-sized balls. Wrap in plastic wrap and refrigerate 15 minutes.

4 Meanwhile, make the stew. Heat vegetable oil in a large saucepan over medium-low heat. Add the onions and sauté 2 minutes. Add the carrots and sauté 5 minutes.

5 Add the chicken or vegetable stock, honey, lemon juice, cinnamon, and dried fruit. Salt and pepper to taste.

6 Gently place the chilled dumplings in the stew. Simmer uncovered over low heat 45 minutes.

Mama says...
Just before serving, dust the stew with a bit of cinnamon.

Lekach

One of the major topics of conversation at Rosh Hashanah is what honey cake recipe to make. Well, this will certainly keep the family happy. It is my favorite classic recipe, and it produces a wonderful cake that is richly spiced with ginger, cinnamon, and other spices. Although it's customary to eat apples and honey during Rosh Hashanah, my family seems driven to eat them together in as many ways as possible. For this reason, my honey cake even features apple juice! Although this cake may be eaten right away, I find that its flavor improves if it's allowed to sit at room temperature at least 3 days before eating. I always make two batches of this recipe—I serve one cake for tea during Rosh Hashanah, and I freeze the other, to be used later for breaking the Yom Kippur fast.

PAREVE: contains no meat or dairy products / must be made 2 weeks in advance
can be frozen up to 1 month
PREPARATION TIME: 25 minutes / **COOKING TIME:** 50 minutes / **SERVES:** 6 to 8

**1 tablespoon vegetable oil ◆ 1½ cups all-purpose flour, sifted
3 tablespoons superfine sugar ◆ ½ teaspoon dried ginger ◆ 2 teaspoons cinnamon
1 teaspoon allspice ◆ 1 teaspoon baking soda ◆ ¼ cup vegetable oil ◆ 1 cup honey
Zest of 1 medium organic orange ◆ 3 large eggs, lightly beaten ◆ ¼ cup apple juice**

◆

1 Preheat the oven to 350°F. Grease with vegetable oil and line a 9-inch by 5-inch loaf pan.

2 In a large bowl, combine the flour, sugar, ginger, cinnamon, allspice, and baking soda.

3 Add the vegetable oil, honey, orange zest, eggs, and apple juice. Beat until smooth. Pour into the pan.

4 Bake 50 minutes or until a toothpick inserted into the center of the cake comes out clean. Remove from the oven and let cool to room temperature in the pan.

5 Tightly wrap the cooled cake in aluminum foil and let sit 2 to 3 days at room temperature, to allow flavors to blend together.

Cinnamon-Apple Strudel

Apple strudel has been a standard Jewish dessert for decades; it's also good for afternoon tea. True Viennese-style apple strudel is made with fresh dough that is rolled out to a paper-thin consistency. It takes considerable skill and time, but we now have access to prepared phyllo, which offers an easy alternative.

MILCHIK: contains dairy products *or* PAREVE: contains no meat or dairy products
can be made in advance / can be frozen (before baking) up to 2 weeks
PREPARATION TIME: 25 minutes / COOKING TIME: 35 to 40 minutes / SERVES: 6

6 medium Granny Smith apples, peeled, cored, and sliced thinly ◆ 2 tablespoons raisins
2 tablespoons slivered almonds ◆ 2 tablespoons ground almonds ◆ 2 teaspoons lemon juice
2 tablespoons bread crumbs ◆ 3 tablespoons light or dark brown sugar ◆ 1 tablespoon
cinnamon ◆ About 12 sheets phyllo (thawed, if frozen) ◆ 1 cup unsalted butter (milchik) or
margarine, melted ◆ 4 tablespoons slivered almonds, toasted ◆ 1 tablespoon raw sesame seeds

◆

1 Preheat the oven to 400°F. Line a baking tray with parchment paper.

2 In a large bowl, mix together the apples, raisins, slivered and ground almonds, lemon juice, bread crumbs, brown sugar, and cinnamon. Set aside.

3 Place one sheet of phyllo on a work surface. Brush with melted butter or margarine. At each layer, add some toasted almonds. Place another sheet on top and brush with melted butter or margarine. Place one more sheet on top and brush with melted butter or margarine. Repeat three times, so that you have four separate three-sheet stacks.

4 Organize the pastry stacks into a large, overlapping rectangle.

5 Place the filling mixture in the center of the pastry. Roll the short sides of pastry inward. Brush the pastry with butter or margarine and roll together like a parcel.

6 Brush with butter or margarine, completely coating the strudel. Sprinkle with sesame seeds. Place the strudel on the baking tray.

7 Bake 35 to 40 minutes or until the strudel is golden brown.

TABERNACLES
Succot

The week-long festival of Succot begins on the fifth day after Yom Kippur (around September/October). The word *Succot* means "booths" and refers to the makeshift huts, or *succahs*, that the Jews called home during their 40 years of wandering in the wilderness following their escape from Egypt. The walls are normally made of wood or canvas and the whole structure is covered by *sekhakh*, a covering that must be made of material that grows in the ground and has been detached from it—usually sticks, bamboo, and branches. The sekhakh should loosely cover the roof so that people inside the succah can see the sky. Today, Jewish families all over the world build succahs in their backyards and children eagerly decorate them with pictures and seasonal fruits and vegetables. Throughout the festival, it is a requirement of Jewish law that all meals be eaten in the succah, unless it rains heavily, in which case the requirement is suspended!

Despite its biblical origins, it is the Jewish Thanksgiving for some because it is also known as the "Festival of the Harvest." It is a time of rejoicing for the goodness and bounty of the earth; therefore, food plays an important role in its celebration. To symbolize the richness of the harvest, stuffed foods of all kinds are served as both savories and sweet dishes. The most popular are Holishkes (stuffed cabbages—see pages 128 to 129) with ground beef, served with a sweet and sour tomato sauce. In Israel, stuffed eggplant or peppers are filled with rice, tomatoes, and herbs. On the sweeter side, recipes like apple strudels and fruit pies with large platters of the new fruits make popular Succot desserts.

Zucchini-Stuffed Tomatoes

When I was little, my family used to go on "Succah crawls," visiting friends and having something to eat in their succahs. Today, my children bring their friends, and this recipe is one of their favorites. When I know that there will be several visitors, I fill smaller tomatoes with the stuffing and serve this as part of a buffet.

MILCHIK: contains dairy products *or* **PAREVE**: contains no meat or dairy products
can be made in advance / **PREPARATION TIME:** 15 minutes / **COOKING TIME:** 15 minutes
SERVES: 4 (as an appetizer) or 2 (as a main course)

2 medium zucchini ◆ 2 tablespoons olive oil
2 cups coarsely chopped cremini or brown cap mushrooms
2 teaspoons fresh, grated, and peeled ginger ◆ 4 large garlic cloves, peeled and crushed
1 cup bread crumbs ◆ ¼ cup ground almonds
1 cup soft goat cheese (milchik) or nondairy cream cheese substitute (pareve)
¼ cup pine nuts ◆ Salt ◆ Freshly ground black pepper ◆ 4 medium beefsteak tomatoes

◆

1 Preheat the oven to 350°F.

2 Grate the zucchini. Place between paper towels and squeeze to remove any excess water.

3 Heat the olive oil in a large saucepan over medium heat. Add the zucchini, mushrooms, ginger, and garlic. Sauté 3 minutes. Drain off any liquid in the pan.

4 Transfer the mixture to a large bowl. Add the bread crumbs, almonds, goat cheese or cream cheese substitute, and pine nuts. Generously salt and pepper to taste.

5 Slice off the tops of the tomatoes. Scoop out and discard the cores and seeds.

6 Gently stuff the tomatoes with the zucchini mixture. Place the tomato "lids" back on top of the tomatoes.

7 Bake 10 to 15 minutes or until the stuffing is golden brown.

Holishkes

*Stuffed cabbage leaves are a traditional dish that is used to celebrate Succot.
My contemporary twist—chopped apricots—provides a nice contrast to the
sweet-and-sour sauce. Serve this as part of a Succot buffet or as a
first course in a Yom Tov meal.*

FLEISHIK: contains meat / can be made in advance
PREPARATION TIME: 35 minutes (plus 30 minutes to chill)
COOKING TIME: 2 hours / **SERVES:** 8 to 10

STUFFED CABBAGE LEAVES

3½ pounds lean ground beef or lamb ♦ ½ cup long-grain white rice
2 medium yellow onions, peeled and chopped finely ♦ ½ cup finely chopped dried apricots
5 large garlic cloves, peeled and chopped finely ♦ 1 teaspoon salt
1 teaspoon freshly ground black pepper ♦ 2 large eggs, lightly beaten ♦ 3 tablespoons water
16 large white or savoy cabbage leaves (select thick leaves in perfect condition)

SWEET-AND-SOUR SAUCE

Two 14-ounce cans diced tomatoes with juice ♦ 2 medium yellow onions, chopped coarsely
1 cup dark raisins (if desired) ♦ 3 tablespoons light brown sugar
2 tablespoons lemon juice ♦ 2 tablespoons ketchup ♦ 1 cup dry red wine ♦ Salt
2 teaspoons cinnamon ♦ Freshly ground black pepper ♦ ½ cup pine nuts, toasted, to garnish

♦

1 In a large bowl, combine the beef or lamb, rice, onions, apricots, garlic, salt, and pepper. (For a smoother mixture, pulse the ingredients in a food processor.) In a small bowl, beat together the eggs and water. Add to the meat mixture and combine. Refrigerate the mixture covered for 30 minutes.

2 Fill a large saucepan with water. Bring to a boil. Plunge the cabbage leaves in the boiling water. Blanch 2 minutes. Transfer the cabbage leaves to a colander and rinse immediately with cold water—this will prevent them from continuing to cook.

3 Transfer the cabbage leaves to a work surface. Using a sharp knife, carefully remove any hard stalks, while doing minimal damage to the leaves.

4 Preheat the oven to 300°F.

5 Shape the chilled beef mixture into egg-sized ovals. Wrap each oval in one or two cabbage leaves, folding and overlapping the leaves so the mixture is completely enclosed in a tight parcel.

6 Place stuffed cabbage leaves in a baking dish.

7 In a medium bowl, mix together all the sauce ingredients. Pour over the stuffed cabbage leaves.

8 Cover the dish. Bake 2 hours.

9 Gently transfer the stuffed cabbage leaves to a serving dish. Spoon the sauce over the stuffed cabbage leaves. Sprinkle with pine nuts and serve.

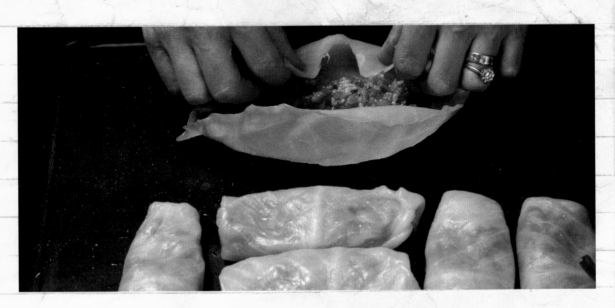

CHANUKAH

Festival of Dedication/Festival of Lights

This winter festival celebrates a great Jewish military victory by the Maccabee army against the Hellenistic occupiers of the land of Israel around 150 B.C. It also celebrates a major miracle: when the Jews recaptured the sacred oil in the temple in Jerusalem, there was only enough holy oil to light the candelabra for one day. Amazingly, however, the candelabra burned for eight days, until new supplies of holy oil were obtained. To commemorate the miracle of the oil, lots of fried foods such as Latkes (see opposite) are eaten at Chanukah. Although it is reported that the Maccabee soldiers ate latkes on the battlefields, they were not the latkes of today, as potatoes were not available until the sixteenth century. They were most likely made from cheese, vegetables, or fruits.

All Jewish homes have a menorah—a nine-stick candelabra. In ancient times, olive oil was used in Chanukah menorahs, but over time, the oil has been replaced by colorful candles, and cards and gifts are exchanged by the family.

Each day of Chanukah is a celebration of the greatness and growth of the miracle. So on the first night, one light is lit and another one on each successive night until the eighth night, when all the lights are lit. Candles are placed in the menorah from right to left, but lit from left to right. The ninth candle is also slightly higher than the others and is known as the Shamash, or servant. It is used to light the other candles.

This festival is a wonderfully joyful occasion for all the family. It tends to fall around Christmastime; as a result, it has become very commercialized.

Latkes

These potato pancakes, called Latkes, are most often enjoyed at Chanukah, when the family gathers together to light the menorah candles, exchange gifts, and play Chanukah games. I like to make "mini" pancakes, which the children love to dip into apple sauce. Latkes are not just for Chanukah, however. They go well with most meals, including roast chicken, cold meats, fried fish, and breakfasts or brunches that include fried eggs. Eat them sweet, sprinkled with superfine sugar and topped with applesauce and sour cream (milchik) or nondairy sour cream substitute (pareve).

PAREVE: contains no meat or dairy products / Passover-friendly
Can be made in advance / can be frozen up to 1 month
PREPARATION TIME: 20 minutes / **COOKING TIME:** 15 minutes / **MAKES:** 10 to 12

**5 boiling potatoes, peeled ◆ 1 small yellow onion, peeled ◆ 2 large eggs, lightly beaten
3 tablespoons fine-ground matzah meal (or self-rising flour, during times other than Passover)
Salt ◆ Freshly ground black pepper ◆ About 4 cups vegetable oil**

◆

1 Grate the potatoes and onions. Place between paper towels. Squeeze to remove excess water. Transfer to dry paper towels and squeeze again.

2 Place the potatoes and onions in a large bowl. Stir in the eggs and matzah meal. Generously salt and pepper to taste.

3 Pour enough vegetable oil in a large, shallow frying pan to create a ½-inch-thick layer of oil. Heat over medium heat.

4 Drop spoonfuls of batter into the hot oil. Do not overcrowd the pan—pancakes may be fried in batches, if necessary. Fry until golden brown on the bottoms (about 4 minutes).

5 Turn the pancakes and fry until golden brown on the other sides (about 3 minutes).

6 Transfer the pancakes to paper towels to absorb excess oil. Serve.

PURIM
Festival of Lots

This joyous festival celebrates the overthrowing of a plot by Haman—a wicked advisor to the king of Persia—to kill all the Jews of the land of Persia. The story of Purim is recounted in *The Megillah*, and is known as the story of Esther. Esther was a young Jewish woman who caught the eye of the king and married him and made him very happy. However, her uncle Mordechai overheard Haman plotting to kill all the Jews and destabilize the country. Mordechai reported it to the king and Esther saved her people.

So Purim is a time of feasting and carnival—gifts of food are exchanged, people wear fancy clothes, and everyone has a ball!

Though synagogues are mostly solemn places, the atmosphere changes at this time of year as children dress up as their favorite Purim characters and make huge amounts of noise at every mention of Haman's name in the telling of the story from *The Megillah*.

The focus is on vegetarian food, including nuts, seeds, and legumes, as this was the diet that the Jewish queen Esther ate in the nonkosher palace of the king. It was her way of keeping the laws of kashrut in a non-Jewish world. Bobs (chickpeas) and nahit (black-eyed peas) dusted with paprika, and Hamantachen—the three-pointed biscuits that symbolize Haman's ears (see pages 134–137)—are often served during Purim.

Fritlach

This recipe for Fritlach, fried pastries, comes from my friend Simone's grandmother—another true Jewish mama! Fritlach is the generic Yiddish word for anything fried, and Simone's grandmother used to fry these during Purim. Simone's mother and her sister had Purim parties, and the fritlach were the highlight! Resembling half moons, these fragile golden bubbles are meant to represent Haman's ears (Hamans Ohren).

PAREVE: contains no meat or dairy products / can be made in advance / can be frozen up to 1 month
PREPARATION TIME: 10 minutes (plus 30 minutes to rest) / **COOKING TIME:** 15 minutes
MAKES: about 40 pastries

**2 large eggs ◆ 1¼ cups all-purpose flour ◆ 2 tablespoons, plus 1 cup vegetable oil
2 to 3 tablespoons superfine sugar**

◆

1 In a food processor that is fitted with a dough blade, process the eggs, flour, and 2 tablespoons vegetable oil until combined. Process the mixture to make a soft dough, gradually adding a bit more water if necessary. (The dough should clean the bowl.)

2 Transfer the dough to a work surface and knead until smooth. Wrap the dough in plastic wrap and refrigerate 30 minutes.

3 Lightly flour a work surface. Remove the dough from the plastic wrap and roll out as thin as possible. Using a cutter or a glass, cut the dough into 3¼-inch circles. Cut each circle in half to form half moons.

4 Allow the dough shapes to dry (they should be dry, but not brittle). To speed up the process, either place the shapes near a window on a sunny day or use a hair dryer to dry the shapes.

5 Pour enough vegetable oil in a large, shallow frying pan to create a ½-inch-thick layer of oil. Heat over medium heat.

6 Gently place the dough shapes in hot oil (do not overcrowd the pan; fry the dough in batches). Turning once or twice, fry until very pale golden yellow (about 4 seconds). Transfer the fried dough to paper towels to blot any excess oil. While the pastries are still hot, dust them with sugar.

Hamantachen with Poppy Seeds

These classic triangular Purim delicacies are filled with poppy seeds, prunes, or apricot preserves. The fillings in hamantachen are hidden—this symbolizes the belief that God always has a plan for the Jews, even if they themselves can not always see it clearly. The triangular shape symbolizes Haman's hat, and the size can vary quite considerably, from small, cocktail-sized morsels to large, heavy treats. Hamantachen can be made with either sweet yeast dough or cookie dough. Both varieties are delicious, but most families have a "tradition" of making one or the other. This recipe uses yeast dough; the next calls for shortbread pastry dough.
Try them both and see which you prefer!

MILCHIK: contains dairy products *or* **PAREVE:** contains no meat or dairy products can be made in advance / **PREPARATION TIME:** 30 minutes (plus 2 hours to allow dough to rise and 10 minutes for mixture to cool) / **COOKING TIME:** 15 minutes / **MAKES:** 40 small pastries

DOUGH
1½ cups warm water, divided ◆ 2 tablespoons active dry yeast
2 teaspoons salt ◆ 8 tablespoons sugar, divided ◆ 2 large eggs
½ cup unsalted butter (milchik) or margarine (pareve)
1 teaspoon vanilla extract ◆ 6 cups bread flour

FILLING
1 cup poppy seeds ◆ ¼ cup water ◆ ½ cup white raisins
1 tablespoon corn syrup ◆ 1 tablespoon superfine sugar

GLAZE
2 tablespoons honey ◆ 2 teaspoons warm water

◆

1 Make the dough. In a medium bowl, mix together ½ cup warm water, the yeast, salt, and 2 tablespoons sugar. Let sit until the mixture becomes foamy (about 10 minutes).

2 Place the eggs, butter or margarine, vanilla extract, and remaining sugar in a food processor fitted with a dough blade. Process to blend. Add the flour and yeast mixture. Process until the mixture is smooth and well combined (about 5 minutes).

3 Transfer the dough to a large bowl, cover with a clean kitchen towel, and let sit about 2 hours, until the dough has doubled in size.

4 Lightly flour a work surface. Transfer the dough to a work surface and roll out to a ¼-inch-thick sheet. Using a cutter or a glass, cut 3-inch circles in the dough.

5 Make the filling. Place all the filling ingredients in a medium saucepan and heat over medium-low heat. Simmer, stirring occasionally, until the liquid has been absorbed and the filling thickens (about 5 minutes).

6 Cool the filling for 10 minutes before using. Place 1 tablespoon filling in the center of each dough circle.

7 Fold the edges of the dough over the filling to form little triangles.

8 Make the glaze. In a small bowl, combine the honey and warm water. Brush the glaze onto all the pastries.

9 Line 2 baking trays with parchment paper. Place the pastries on the trays. Let sit 30 minutes to rise.

10 Preheat the oven to 350°F.

11 Bake the pastries 15 minutes or until golden brown.

Mama says...
Just before serving, dust the pastries with confectioners' sugar.

Hamantachen with Apple

*Fans of shortbread will love these delicious treats. The filling combines apples,
walnuts, and raisins for a rich, tasty complement to the subtly sweet pastry dough.*

MILCHIK: contains dairy products *or* **PAREVE:** contains no meat or dairy products
can be made in advance / can be frozen up to 1 month / **PREPARATION TIME:** 30 minutes
COOKING TIME: 15 to 20 minutes / **MAKES:** about 30 small pastries

DOUGH
2¼ cups all-purpose flour ◆ ½ cup unsalted butter (milchik) or margarine (pareve)
Zest of 1 medium organic lemon ◆ 2 teaspoons lemon juice ◆ 1 large egg
3 tablespoons superfine sugar

FILLING
3 tablespoons white raisins ◆ ¼ cup chopped walnuts
¼ cup unsalted butter (milchik) or margarine (pareve) ◆ ¼ packed cup light brown sugar
1 teaspoon cinnamon ◆ 1 medium red or green sweet apple, peeled

GLAZE AND TOPPING
White of 1 large egg, lightly whisked ◆ 2 tablespoons poppy seeds
2 tablespoons decorative cake sprinkles

◆

1 Make the dough. Place all the ingredients in a
food processor that is fitted with a dough blade.
Process until a dough is formed.

2 Remove the dough from the processor and
wrap in plastic wrap. Flatten the dough to
½-inch thick. Refrigerate for 30 minutes. Clean
the processor bowl.

3 Meanwhile, make the filling. Place the raisins,
walnuts, butter or margarine, brown sugar, and
cinnamon in the food processor. Pulse gently
until the ingredients are combined.

4 Grate the apples. Place between paper towels
and squeeze any excess water from the apples.
Stir the apples into the raisin-nut mixture.

5 Preheat the oven to 400°F.

6 Lightly flour a work surface. Remove the dough from the plastic wrap and roll out to a ¼-inch-thick sheet. Using a 3-inch cutter or a glass, cut circles into the dough.

7 Place about 1 teaspoon of the raisin-nut mixture in the center of each circle.

8 Fold the edges of the dough over the filling to form little triangles.

9 Line two baking trays with parchment paper. Place the pastries on the trays and glaze with the egg white. Sprinkle with poppy seeds and decorative cake sprinkles.

10 Bake 15 to 20 minutes, until golden brown.

PASSOVER

Pesach

Passover is an exciting time of year, especially for children, and it includes many time-honored rituals. A thorough "spring cleaning" of the house helps to symbolize (and achieve) an atmosphere of freshness and renewal. This is the oldest Jewish festival, and it marks the flight of the Israelites from slavery in Egypt into freedom. They left in such a hurry that their bread did not have time to rise. Thus, for eight days a year, Jews eat only unleavened foods.

During the first two nights of Passover, in a service performed at home called Seder, Jews retell the story of the exodus. This is followed by a meal full of symbolic foods. The Seder plate contains foods with special meaning: Charoset (a mixture of chopped walnuts, wine, cinnamon, and apples; see page 141) represents the mortar the Jewish slaves used to assemble the pharaoh's bricks; parsley (symbolizing springtime) is dipped in salt water to remind us of the tears of the Jewish slaves; eggs are a symbol of spring and the cycle of life; shank bones are symbolic of the sacrificial lamb offering; and bitter herbs such as grated horseradish reflect the bitter affliction of slavery.

During the Seder, four glasses of wine are poured to represent the four stages of the exodus: freedom, deliverance, redemption, and release. A fifth cup of wine, the Cup of Elijah, is poured and placed on the Seder table as an offering for the prophet Elijah. The door to the home is opened to invite in the prophet Elijah.

There are many strict rules surrounding Passover: only special Passover foods, utensils, and dishware are allowed and none of them should be used at other times of year. Similarly, when buying in supermarkets, only foods that are specially marked "Kosher for Passover" are permitted, as they have been supervised and kept away from any hint of leavened foods or grain. During Passover, Coconut Pyramids (see page 147), Cinnamon Balls (see page 148), and My Almond Macaroons (see page 145) are all created in accordance with the prohibition against leavened products.

Dried Fruit Compote

The most difficult meal during Passover is breakfast. I think this is because we have become so accustomed to eating bread, toast, cereals, rolls, and other flour-based foods, which are prohibited at this time. Passover cereals are available, but they are not very satisfying. Matzah meal and butter are delicious, but they are not very filling or nutritious. My mother solved the "Passover breakfast" dilemma by serving a large bowl of this delicious compote. Served with ice cream or sponge cake, this also makes a good dessert.

PAREVE: contains no meat or dairy products / Passover-friendly / can be made in advance
PREPARATION TIME: 10 minutes (plus at least 2 hours to chill) / **COOKING TIME:** 0 minutes
SERVES: 4

1⅓ cups raisins and currants ◆ ½ cup dried cherries
½ cup white raisins ◆ 10 dried pitted prunes ◆ 10 dried apricots
About 2 cups hot, freshly brewed fragrant tea (such as Earl Grey or jasmine)
2 tablespoons sugar ◆ 1 medium lemon, sliced

1 Place the dried fruits in a medium bowl and cover with hot tea. Add sugar and lemon slices.

2 Cover the bowl with a plate. Set aside to cool to room temperature.

3 Refrigerate uncovered for at least 2 hours (and preferably overnight).

Mama says...
For a tasty Passover breakfast, serve this with plain yogurt and a bit of honey. For a tasty Passover dessert, stir in about 1/4 cup Passover-friendly liqueur.

Charoset

This fruit and wine pâté is one of the symbolic foods that we have on the Passover Seder table. It represents the mortar with which the Jews were forced to make bricks when they built the cities of Pithom and Ramses for their Egyptian taskmasters. The word "Charoset" means clay in Hebrew. This is a classic Ashkenazi dish that combines apples, walnuts, cinnamon, kiddush wine, and sugar. Charoset is a good example of a dish that varies according to the country in which it's made and the local ingredients that are available. Middle Eastern Jews tend to make Charoset with dates, dried apricots, and raisins. I like to make a large bowl of Charoset, and I hide the leftovers, as I thoroughly enjoy having some of it for breakfast the morning after Seder night. This chunkier version of Charoset includes lemon, which represents the sourness of slavery, and dates, which represent the sweetness of freedom.

PAREVE: contains no meat or dairy products / Passover-friendly / can be made in advance
PREPARATION TIME: 10 minutes / **COOKING TIME:** 10 minutes / **SERVES:** 8 to 10

**1 cup almonds ◆ 6 red or green, sweet apples, peeled, cored, and chopped coarsely
1 cup coarsely chopped pitted dates ◆ 1 teaspoon cinnamon
Zest and juice of 1 medium organic lemon ◆ ⅓ cup kiddush Passover-friendly red wine**

---

1 Preheat the oven to 400°F. Place the almonds on a baking tray. Bake 10 minutes. Remove from the oven and let cool.

2 In a large bowl, mix together the apples, dates, and almonds.

3 Stir in cinnamon, zest, lemon juice, and wine.

4 Cover the bowl. Refrigerate until chilled.

5 Transfer the chilled mixture to a serving bowl and serve.

Matzah Omelet

This is a very popular Passover breakfast, light lunch, or supper dish among Ashkenazi Jews. My children like these sweet, so I top them with sugar. For a savory omelet, top them with salt instead. Serve these with applesauce and sour cream, and a dusting of cinnamon.

PAREVE: contains no meat or dairy products / Passover-friendly / can be made in advance
PREPARATION TIME: 10 minutes / **COOKING TIME:** 5 minutes / **SERVES:** 2 to 3

**6 large, plain matzah broken into bite-sized pieces ◆ 5 large eggs, lightly beaten
2 teaspoons salt ◆ 3 tablespoons vegetable oil**

1 Place the matzah crackers in a large bowl. Cover with cold water. Let sit 2 to 3 minutes. Drain. Add the eggs and salt to the crackers and mix well.

2 Heat vegetable oil in a medium frying pan over medium heat. Add the matzah mixture and fry until the bottom of the mixture is golden brown (about 2 minutes).

3 Using a spatula, break up the omelet into pieces. Turning frequently, fry until the pieces are crisp and browned on all sides (about 3 minutes). (The pieces will continue to break as they are turned.)

*Mama says...
Sprinkle with salt or sugar and serve immediately with applesauce and sour cream.*

Boobelach

It's tradition to serve boobelach for breakfast or as a snack during Passover, but they may be enjoyed at any time of the year. My mother makes these pancakes for my children every Sunday. Early Sunday mornings I drive to her house, where she is waiting for me with the pancakes all wrapped up in a napkin. My children eat them in the car on their way to Cheder (Sunday school).

MILCHIK: contains dairy products / Passover-friendly
PREPARATION TIME: 10 minutes / **COOKING TIME:** 10 minutes / **MAKES:** 12 pancakes

**3 large eggs ◆ 1 teaspoon salt ◆ 4 tablespoons fine-ground matzah meal
(or cake flour or self-rising flour, during times other than Passover) ◆ ¼ cup milk
About 2 to 3 tablespoons vegetable oil**

◆

1 In a medium bowl, whisk together the eggs and salt until the mixture is light and fluffy. Stir in the matzah meal and milk.

2 Heat the vegetable oil in a large frying pan over medium heat.

3 Drop tablespoons of the mixture in hot oil (do not overcrowd the pan; pancakes may be fried in batches). Turning once, fry until golden brown on both sides (about 2 to 3 minutes per side).

4 Place the pancakes on paper towels, then transfer to a serving plate and serve immediately.

Mama says...
I like my pancakes light and fluffy, so during times other than Passover, I make them with cake flour or self-rising flour. Many, however, prefer the Passover-friendly, heavier matzah meal all year round.

My Almond Macaroons

Passover is not quite Passover unless my family is munching on almond macaroons—the traditional favorite treat of this festival. This recipe uses coarsely chopped almonds as well as ground almonds, and brown sugar instead of white sugar—which makes them a little different than my mother's macaroons. This recipe works well with pecans, too. These may be frozen, or they may be stored in an airtight container at room temperature for up to 5 days.

PAREVE: contains no meat or dairy products / Passover-friendly
can be made in advance / can be frozen up to 1 month
PREPARATION TIME: 10 minutes / **COOKING TIME:** 20 minutes / **MAKES:** about 48 macaroons

2 cups ground almonds ◆ ¼ cup whole almonds, chopped coarsely
1 packed cup light brown sugar ◆ 1 teaspoon vanilla extract ◆ Whites of 5 large eggs
½ teaspoon salt ◆ About 48 almond halves (about 2 ounces total)

◆

1 Preheat the oven to 375°F. Line two baking sheets with parchment paper. Set aside.

2 In a large bowl, mix together the ground almonds, chopped almonds, brown sugar, and vanilla extract.

3 Place the egg whites and salt in a medium bowl. Whisk together until the egg whites are stiff, but not dry.

4 Stir the egg whites into the nut mixture, a tablespoon at a time, until the nut mixture is stiff, but not too wet. (Some egg whites may be left over—discard any that remain.)

5 Gently drop 1 tablespoon of the mixture, spaced about 1 inch apart, onto the baking sheets. Push one almond half onto the top of each macaroon, flattening the macaroons slightly.

6 Bake 20 minutes or until the macaroons are golden brown and just set. (The macaroons will harden as they cool.)

7 Transfer to a cooling rack and let cool.

Matzah Pudding

My family often requests this dessert for our family get-together for Seder. It's delicious and generously sized, and it contains all the flavors of Passover (such as ground almonds, cinnamon, lemon, and apples). It can be eaten hot or cold, and it keeps well, making it an ideal Shabbat dessert as well.

PAREVE: contains no meat or dairy products / Passover-friendly
can be made in advance / can be frozen up to 2 weeks
PREPARATION TIME: 30 minutes / **COOKING TIME:** 50 minutes / **SERVES:** 8 to 10

8 large, plain matzah broken into bite-sized pieces ◆ ½ cup boiling water
3 red or green apples, peeled and grated ◆ ½ cup dark raisins
½ cup coarsely chopped dried apricots
½ cup coarsely chopped walnuts or almonds ◆ 4 tablespoons fine-ground matzah meal
5 tablespoons, plus 1 teaspoon superfine sugar, divided ◆ 2 teaspoons cinnamon
½ teaspoon freshly grated nutmeg ◆ 2 tablespoons honey
Juice and zest of 1 medium organic lemon ◆ 4 large eggs
2 tablespoons margarine, melted ◆ 4 tablespoons apricot jam ◆ 1 tablespoon water

◆

1 Preheat the oven to 325°F. Grease and line a 9-inch square or round baking pan. Set aside.

2 Place the matzah crackers and boiling water in a medium bowl. Let sit 5 minutes. Drain. Place the crackers between paper towels and squeeze out any excess water.

3 Place the soaked crackers in a large bowl. Add the apples, raisins, apricots, walnuts or almonds, matzah meal, 1 tablespoon superfine sugar, cinnamon, nutmeg, honey, zest, and lemon juice.

4 In a separate bowl, whisk together the eggs and remaining superfine sugar until the mixture is light and fluffy. Add to the matzah mixture. Add the margarine. Mix well and pour into the pan.

5 Bake 50 minutes or until a knife inserted in the center of the mixture comes out clean.

6 Place the jam and water in a small saucepan. Cook over low heat 3 minutes, stirring frequently. Brush the jam glaze onto the dessert. Let sit at least 10 minutes before serving.

Coconut Pyramids

These are pyramid-shaped treats that represent the pyramids that the Israelites built for the Egyptians. My mother taught me to get the shape right by using an egg cup, but I have found that molding the treats by hand is quicker and easier. These may be frozen, or they may be stored in an airtight container at room temperature for up to 5 days.

PAREVE: contains no meat or dairy products / Passover-friendly
can be made in advance / can be frozen up to 1 month
PREPARATION TIME: 15 minutes / **COOKING TIME:** 15 minutes / **MAKES:** 24 pyramids

2 large eggs ◆ ¾ cup superfine sugar
Zest and juice of 1 medium organic lemon ◆ 3¾ cups shredded coconut

◆

1 Preheat the oven to 375°F. Line a baking tray with parchment paper.

2 In a large bowl, whisk together the eggs and sugar until the mixture is thick and creamy. Stir in the zest, lemon juice, and coconut. Mix well.

3 Using wet hands, shape about 1 tablespoon mixture into a pyramid. Repeat using all the mixture. Place the pyramids on the tray.

4 Bake 15 to 20 minutes or until the pyramids are lightly browned.

Mama says...
Sprinkle shredded coconut on a serving plate.
Decoratively arrange the pyramids on the plate.

Cinnamon Balls

I seem to spend more time in the kitchen at Passover than at any other time of the year. A good part of this time is spent baking. The cakes and pastries are fantastic, but they're somewhat labor-intensive. That's where the children come in handy! I prepare the mixture and they roll out the dough, so baking is done in next to no time.

PAREVE: contains no meat or dairy products / Passover-friendly
can be made in advance / can be frozen up to 1 month
PREPARATION TIME: 25 minutes / **COOKING TIME:** 15 minutes / **MAKES:** 20 balls

**2 cups ground almonds ◆ 1 cup superfine sugar
1 tablespoon, plus 1 teaspoon cinnamon, divided ◆ Whites of 2 large eggs
½ cup confectioners' sugar**

◆

1 Preheat the oven to 325°F. Line a baking tray with parchment paper. Set aside.

2 In a medium bowl, combine the almonds, superfine sugar, and 1 tablespoon cinnamon. Set aside.

3 In a small, clean bowl, whisk the egg whites until they form soft peaks.

4 Stir the egg whites, a tablespoon at a time, into the almond-sugar mixture until the mixture is stiff. (Some egg whites may be left over—discard any that remain.)

5 Using wet hands, shape the mixture into small balls. Arrange 1 inch apart on the tray.

6 Bake until golden brown (about 15 minutes).

7 Meanwhile, place the confectioners' sugar and remaining cinnamon in a small bowl. Mix well.

8 Remove the baked pastries from the oven. Roll each ball in the sugar-cinnamon mixture and place on a cooling rack. Let cool.

9 Roll the cooled balls in the sugar-cinnamon mixture again. Serve.

Plava

This light, lemon-flavored sponge cake is traditionally made during Passover, when Jews are not permitted to eat foods made with flour. The most common substitutes used during this time are potato flour, matzah meal, and cake meal. Although this recipe calls for a lemon glaze, the cake may also be served plain or with Dried Fruit Compote (see page 139) or ice cream.

PAREVE: contains no meat or dairy products / Passover-friendly
can be made in advance / can be frozen up to 1 month
PREPARATION TIME: 25 minutes / COOKING TIME: 40 minutes / SERVES: 6 to 8

CAKE
1 tablespoon vegetable oil ◆ 6 large eggs, divided ◆ 1 cup superfine sugar, divided
¾ cup fine-ground matzah meal ◆ ¼ cup ground almonds
½ teaspoon cinnamon ◆ Grated zest and juice of 1 medium organic lemon
3 tablespoons slivered almonds

GLAZE
¾ cup superfine sugar ◆ ¼ cup water ◆ Grated zest and juice of 1 medium organic lemon

◆

1 Preheat the oven to 350°F. Grease with vegetable oil and line an 8½-inch square springform cake pan. Set aside.

2 Make the cake. Place the egg yolks and sugar in the bowl of an electric mixer. Mix 3 to 5 minutes, until thick and smooth.

3 In a medium bowl, whisk the egg whites until soft peaks form. Gradually add the remaining sugar, beating well after each addition, until the mixture forms stiff peaks. Set aside.

4 In a medium bowl, combine the matzah meal, ground almonds, cinnamon, zest, and lemon juice. Fold into the egg yolk mixture.

5 Using a metal spoon, fold 1 tablespoon egg white mixture into the egg yolk mixture. Gently stir the remaining egg white mixture into the egg yolk mixture.

6 Pour the batter into the pan. Sprinkle with slivered almonds.

7 Bake 40 minutes or until the cake is golden brown and a toothpick inserted into the center of the cake comes out clean.

8 Remove from the oven and let cool in the pan. (The cake may sink a bit.)

9 Make the glaze. Place the sugar and water in a small saucepan. Bring to a boil over medium-high heat. Reduce the heat to medium-low and simmer 4 minutes.

10 Stir in the zest and lemon juice.

11 Drizzle the glaze, 1 tablespoon at a time, over the cooled cake. Take the cake out of the cake pan to serve.

◆

SHAVUOT
Pentecost/Festival of Weeks

Shavuot, the Feast of the Weeks, is the Jewish holiday celebrating the harvest season in Israel. Shavuot, which means "weeks," refers to the timing of the festival that is held exactly seven weeks after Passover. Shavuot also commemorates the anniversary of the giving of the Torah and the Ten Commandments to Moses and the Israelites at Mount Sinai.

It is customary on Shavuot to decorate the home and synagogue with fruits, flowers, and greens, as the first fruits of the new season were harvested around Shavuot in the days of the Temple. In addition, the sages say that although Mount Sinai was situated in a desert, the mountain bloomed and sprouted flowers when the Ten Commandments were given to Moses.

There is also the custom of eating dairy foods on Shavuot. Therefore, recipes like Cheesecake (see pages 154 to 155) and Cheese Blintzes (see opposite) are popular. There are a number of reasons for this custom: with the giving of the Torah, the Jews became obligated to observe the laws of Kashruth. As the Torah was given on Shabbat, no cattle could be slaughtered nor could utensils be koshered (in hot water, etc.), so they could only eat dairy products.

Classic Cheese Blintzes

*These treats go by many names: the French call them crepes, the Russians call them
blini, and the Jews call them blintzes. They are very thin, crepelike pancakes that
are filled with cream cheese or cottage cheese and even fruit.*

MILCHIK: contains dairy products / can be made in advance / can be frozen up to 1 month
PREPARATION TIME: 20 minutes / **COOKING TIME:** 20 minutes / **MAKES:** 8 blintzes

PANCAKES

1 cup self-rising flour ◆ 1 large egg ◆ 1 cup milk ◆ 1 teaspoon salt
2 to 3 tablespoons sunflower or vegetable oil

FILLING

1 cup cream cheese, softened ◆ 1 large egg ◆ Zest of 1 medium organic lemon
1 tablespoon superfine sugar

◆

1 Lay a large (12 inches by 12 inches) sheet of parchment paper on a work surface. Set aside.

2 Make the batter. In a blender or a large bowl, combine the flour, egg, milk, and salt until smooth.

3 Heat the sunflower oil in an 8-inch skillet over medium heat. Pour 3 tablespoons batter into the hot oil. Tilt the pan so the mixture covers the pan in a thin, even layer. Cook until the batter sets and the pancake edges begin to lift (about 2 minutes).

4 Flip the pancake onto the other side and cook about 10 seconds. Gently transfer the pancake to the parchment paper. Repeat, heating more oil in the pan as needed, until the batter is used. Avoid overlapping the pancakes on the parchment paper; instead, stack them. Reserve the pan for later use.

5 Make the filling. Place all the ingredients in a medium bowl and combine well. Place 1 tablespoon filling in the center of each pancake. Fold 2 opposite sides of the pancake over the filling, then fold the remaining side over those. Roll the pancake to enclose the filling.

6 Pour 1 to 2 tablespoons oil in the pan over medium heat. Fry the blintzes until just golden brown (about 2 minutes). Gently turn the blintzes and cook 1 minute. Serve immediately.

Old-Fashioned Cheesecake

Shavuot is sometimes teasingly referred to as "the cheesecake festival" because of the popularity of this dessert during this festival. Shavuot celebrates the time when God gave the Jews the Ten Commandments and all the laws, including the laws of Lashrus (kosher). Because the Children of Israel were not immediately familiar with all the commandments relating to kashrut, they decided to avoid meat, and they ate only dairy instead. This recipe is both quick and easy to make, and it uses few ingredients.

MILCHIK: contains dairy products / can be made in advance
PREPARATION TIME: 10 minutes (plus about 4 hours to cool) / **COOKING TIME:** 35 minutes
SERVES: 8 to 10

For variety, try making cheesecakes with any of the following:
1 tablespoon lime juice, zest of 2 organic limes, and 2 tablespoons shredded coconut (plus zest of 1 lime and 2 tablespoons shredded coconut for decoration)
1 tablespoon instant coffee
4 tablespoons fresh raspberries (plus raspberries and mint sprigs for decoration)

For this recipe, with chocolate and cinnamon:
CHEESECAKE
1 tablespoon vegetable oil ◆ 3 cups crushed graham crackers
¾ cup unsalted butter or margarine, melted
2 cups cream cheese or large-curd cottage cheese ◆ 2 large eggs
1 cup superfine sugar ◆ ¼ cup finely grated bittersweet chocolate ◆ 2 teaspoons cinnamon

TOPPING
1½ cups sour cream ◆ 2 tablespoons superfine sugar

◆

1 Preheat the oven to 350°F. Grease with vegetable oil and line a 9-inch round (3-inch-deep) springform cake pan.

2 Make the cheesecake. In a medium bowl, mix together the graham cracker crumbs and butter or margarine. Press the mixture in an even layer into the bottom of the pan.

3 In a medium bowl, beat together the cream cheese or cottage cheese, eggs, and sugar. Beat in the chocolate and cinnamon (if making a cheesecake using other the suggested ingredients, beat those in at this time).

4 Pour the mixture over the graham cracker crust in the pan.

5 Bake 30 minutes. Carefully remove from the oven and set aside. Do not turn off the oven.

6 Make the topping. In a small bowl, mix together the sour cream and sugar. Pour over the cake.

7 Return the pan to the oven. Bake 5 minutes.

8 Turn off the oven. Let the cheesecake sit in the oven until it has completely cooled (about 4 hours). Then invert it onto a serving plate.

Glossary

Ashkenazi: Jews originating from Eastern Europe.

Bagel: a doughnut-shaped, yeast-dough, bread roll that is boiled, glazed with egg white, and baked.

Blintz: a thick pancake, Russian in origin and similar to the French crepe, that is stuffed with various fillings and often topped with sour cream.

Booba: a term of endearment for a Jewish grandmother.

Borscht: a Russian-style soup, usually made with beets, that can be served hot or cold, with either sour cream or boiled potatoes.

Cake meal or matzah cake meal: cake meal is very fine matzah meal, perfect for use during Passover when all-purpose flour is prohibited.

Challah: Sabbath bread, traditionally made with egg yeast dough, that is eaten during Sabbaths and festivals.

Chanukah: the festival of lights during which especially foods fried in oil are eaten.

Charoset: A mixture of chopped fruits, nuts, spices, and red wine that is eaten as part of the Passover seder service.

Cheder: Jewish Sunday school.

Cholent: a traditional meat and vegetable stew that is prepared on the eve of the Shabbat, left to cook slowly overnight, and eaten for lunch on the Sabbath.

Chrain: a sauce made of grated horseradish and beets.

Compote: a mixture of dried fruits that are sweetened and cooked.

Falafel: a deep-fried chickpea ball that is served as an appetizer or is stuffed into a pita bread with salad and tahini or hummus.

Fleishik: Food that contains meat.

Gedempte: Stewed or braised.

Gefilte fish: a mixture of ground fish, matzah meal, ground almonds, and eggs, which is shaped into balls and poached or fried.

Haimisher: Jewish homestyle.

Hamantachen: triangular pastries that are usually filled with poppy seeds and jam, prunes, or another similar fruit. These are served during Purim as symbols of the three-cornered hat that Haman used to wear.

Holishkes: cabbage leaves stuffed with meat and rice and baked in a sweet-and-sour sauce.

Hummus: a Middle Eastern dip made from chickpeas and tahini.

Kasha: buckwheat groats, usually served with meat, but also in soups or salads, or as a breakfast cereal.

Kichel: a cookie.

Kiddush: the ritual blessing made over wine at the start of a meal on Sabbaths and festivals to sanctify the day.

Kneidlach: light dumplings made of fine-ground matzah meal and served in chicken soup. (Alternative name for a matzah ball.)

Knish: pastry filled with potatoes, meat, cheese, or rice and baked.

Kosher: "fit to be eaten," according to the laws of the Old Testament.

Kreplach: Pockets of pastalike dough, stuffed with meat or cheese and boiled or fried.

Kugel: a casserole that is usually made with potatoes or noodles, and which may be either sweet or savory.

Latke: a small potato pancake that is traditionally eaten during Chanukah.

Lekach: a dark honey cake that is traditionally served during Rosh Hashanah and after the fast of Yom Kippur.

Lokshen: egg noodles that are usually served in soup or used in kugel.

Mandelbrot: twice-baked almond cookies.

Matzah: unleavened bread, traditionally served during the eight days of Passover.

Menorah: the seven-branched candelabra lit during Chanukah.

Milchik: food that contains dairy products.

Pareve: "neutral" food that contains neither meat nor dairy products and may therefore be eaten with milchik or fleishik foods.

Pareve cream: nondairy cream substitute.

Passover or Pesach: an eight-day festival commemorating the exodus of the Jews from Egypt. Families gather to enjoy lavish meals called Seders.

Pita: a Middle Eastern flat, round bread with a pocket that can be filled with falafel, hummus, tahini, salad, and other ingredients.

Purim: the most festive of the Jewish holidays, with prizes and costumes to celebrate the story of Esther who became the king's wife and foiled a plot to kill all the Jews in the kingdom.

Rosh Hashanah: "the head of the year" when Jews repent their sins and hope for a prosperous new year.

Schmaltz: rendered chicken fat taken from the top of chicken soup.

Seder: a ritual service and meal at the start of Passover, which includes the story of the Jews' exodus from Egypt.

Sephardi: Jews originating from Spain, Morocco, or the Middle East.

Shabbat: the Sabbath (Saturday), the Jewish day of rest. Beginning at sunset, Friday evening, it ends approximately twenty-five hours later.

Shavuot: The Feast of the Weeks occurring seven weeks after the first day of Passover.

Shtetl: a small Jewish settlement in Eastern Europe.

Shtetlach: a small Jewish settlement.

Strudel: a pastry made of very thin sheets of dough, with sweet or savory fillings.

Succot: the jubilant Festival of Tabernacles, which falls five days after Yom Kippur.

Tahini: sesame seed paste that is used as a condiment or as an ingredient in dips.

Tzimmes: carrot stew that is sweetened with honey or sugar.

Varnishkes: bow-shaped noodles that are traditionally served with kasha.

Yom Kippur: the Day of Atonement, the most sacred of Jewish holidays. All work is replaced by prayers and fasting on this day.

Yom Tov: a Jewish festival or High Holy Day.

Index

nuts
    almond macaroons 145
    baklava 98–9
    booba's kiddush kichels 104
    charoset 141
    cinnamon balls 148
    mandelbrot 113
    matzah pudding 146
    old-fashioned fruit cake 114–15

oatmeal cookies 105
old-fashioned cheesecake 154–5
old-fashioned fruit cake 114–15

Passover 138–51
pasta
    kreplach 38–9
    lokshen kugel 97
pea soup, split 31
peaches
    berry-peach salad 94
pearl barley
    barley soup 34
peppers
    goulash 64
    Mediterranean salmon 54
    pickled vegetables 75
    ratatouille 76
pickled tongue or salt beef 68–9
pickled vegetables 75
plava 150–1
plums
    apple-plum crumble 90
pot roast 58
potatoes
    crispy, sliced roast potatoes 79
    croquette potatoes 80
    latkes 131
    potato kugel 74
    potato salad with lemon
        mayonnaise 78
poultry see chicken; turkey
Purim 132–7

raspberries
    berry-peach salad 94
    chocolate pavlova with
        raspberries 95
ratatouille 76
red cabbage with wine 79

rice
    holishkes 128–9
    mushroom rice 73
Rosh Hashanah 118–25

salmon, Mediterranean 54
Shavuot 152–5
smoked trout salad 48
soup croutons 43
soups 28–39
split pea soup 31
stuffed monkey 110–11
Succot 126–9
sweet and sour meatballs 61

tabbouleh 23
Tabernacles 126–9
thick cabbage and bean soup 29
tomatoes
    cholent 66–7
    goulash 64
    meatball sauce 61
    ratatouille 76
    sauce for beef strudel 62–3
    sweet-and-sour sauce 128–9
    zucchini-stuffed tomatoes 127
tongue 68–9
trout 48
turkey schnitzel 59
tzimmes 120–1
vegetables
    pickled vegetables 75
    ratatouille 76
    vegetable couscous 84–5
    vegetable soup 30

zucchini-stuffed tomatoes 127

Passover-friendly index
Use this at-a-glance list to find recipes
suitable for Passover.
Starters:
charoset, 141
egg and onion, 20
eggplant dip, 12
fried eggplant salad, 24
grandma's chopped liver, 21
Soups, Dumplings, and Bread:
borscht, 28
golden vegetable soup, 30
homemade bagels, 44–5
knaidlach or matzah balls, 35
ultimate chicken soup, 36–7
Main Courses:
beef strudel, 62–3
chicken or turkey schnitzel, 59
Friday night roast chicken, 57
fried fish, 49
halibut with egg-lemon sauce, 49
honey-roasted chicken, 119
liver with onions, 69
Mediterranean salmon, 54
mother-in-law's boiled gefilte fish, 50
pickled tongue or salt beef, 68–9
pot roast, 58
sweet and sour meatballs, 61
Side Dishes:
chrain, 72
crispy, sliced roast potatoes, 79
croquette potatoes, 80
homemade coleslaw, 82–3
latkes, 131
pickled vegetables, 75
potato kugel, 74
potato salad with lemon mayonnaise, 78
ratatouille, 76
red cabbage with wine, 79
tzimmes, 120
Desserts and Cakes:
berry-peach salad, 94
boobelach, 143
chocolate roulade, 91
cinnamon balls, 148
coconut pyramids, 147
dried fruit compote, 139
matzah pudding, 146
my almond macaroons, 145
plava, 150–51

Picture Credits

Mama says...
Be careful when grating horseradish as the vapors are very powerful and can make you sneeze, cough, or cry (and that's before you've eaten it!)